THE EVER PRESENT NOW

—— THE ——

Ever
Present
Now

A NEW UNDERSTANDING OF
CONSCIOUSNESS AND PROPHECY

LORI ADAILE TOYE

I AM AMERICA PUBLISHING & DISTRIBUTING
P.O. Box 2511, Payson, Arizona, 85547, USA.
www.iamamerica.com

I AM America Maps and Books have been marketed since 1989 by I AM America Seventh Ray Publishing and Distributing, through workshops, conferences, and numerous bookstores in the United States and internationally. If you are interested in obtaining information on available releases please write or call:
I AM America, P.O. Box 2511, Payson, Arizona, 85547, USA. (480) 744-6188, or visit:

www.iamamerica.com
www.loritoye.com
www.loritoye.org

Graphic Design and Typography by Lori Toye
Editing by Betsy Robinson

Love, in service, breathes the breath for all!

Print On Demand Version

10 9 8 7 6 5 4 3 2 1

Question: "When will the changes begin?"

Response: "The *Time of Change* is *Now*."

CONTENTS

CHAPTER FOUR

Golden Cities 67

CHAPTER FIVE

Spiritual Teachings 109

Introduction

This book represents more than twenty years of articles and notes I have written about my insights regarding the I AM America Teachings. Some of the articles were created to clarify ideas and ideals; others were composed to share information in magazines, newsletters, and for students. When I first began to receive messages from the Spiritual Teachers, I had no inkling or expectation that I was receiving a body of information that would later include extensive teachings on Self-development, Meditation and Decree, the Seven Rays of Light and Sound, Healing, Ascension, the Golden Cities and the Western Shamballa Tradition, and, of course, Prophecy.

The origins of these teachings are the recorded trance-channeled sessions; however, after I am out of the trance state, I rarely remember anything that is spoken. Once the material is transcribed and organized, I'm as surprised as anyone else regarding the content. So, like any other student of these types of teachings, I must absorb the content and form an opinion regarding the material before I express my impressions. Therefore these chapters reflect my personal beliefs and experiences with the information. My teacher, Saint Germain, would call this my "Point of Perception."

Most, if not all, of the information that I receive is a spoken transmission from Spiritual Teachers, such as the aforementioned Saint Germain, while I am in the trance state. The exception is a small portion of automatic writing that I received; a service performed for the Master K. H. A sample of this type of material is the chapter titled "Desire that Co-Creates the Love of God."

For the most part, I prefer trance-channeled, orally received information. This type of channeled material has an unmistaken spirit and purity that is difficult to duplicate by any other means. And this form of channeling is rare. The channel not only transmits information that can be later transcribed and used, but if you happen to sit in on this type of session or listen to a cassette version (analog, not digital) from the I AM America collection, you will feel an inordinate stream of energy and vibration which comes directly from the ethereal planes. This energy is amazingly revitalizing and harmonizing to the human energy field.

My formal experience as a channel first began with a session monitor asking me questions while I was in a deep state of meditation and in contact with the ethereal teachers. I would telepathically relay each question, and then speak aloud the Spiritual Teacher's answer. Each session was recorded. This method was a bit tedious, and I felt like an inter-dimensional telephone. As my ability to relay information further developed, I was able to literally morph my consciousness so that I was ONE with the Spiritual Teachers. I have no doubt that this process was realized through a mutual effort by all of us: the monitor, other students participating in the session, the teachers, and me. For me, it resulted in personal spiritual growth and the practice I received in each session; for the monitor, there was an increase in energy level and ever-evolving receptivity; and for the Spiritual Teachers, only they can say. In those early days I would laughingly tell others that at this juncture, channeling reminded me of the "Vulcan Mind-Meld." However, today I understand that this unique camaraderie is the metaphysical "Oneship" that Kuan Yin and Saint Germain have so patiently described in many of their teachings.

Inevitably my trance process developed into what is commonly known as clairaudient-trance channeling. I've written in detail about this experience in these pages, and I have also covered the venerated custom of the Oral Tradition—the ageless technique of verbally speaking and conveying spiritual knowledge from teacher to student.

As time progressed, it was apparent that we were receiving an array of information and unique knowledge. This included spiritual techniques and advice for self-development alongside information for healing and how to use and access the energies of the Golden Cities. You will find several chapters on the Golden Cities and how they are structured—both physically and spiritually. This includes relevant teachings regarding their unique provenance and the etymology of their names—spoken in "Owaspee," the language of the angels.

Since 1992, my husband and I have had the privilege to live in the mountainous expanse of the Golden City of Gobean (which contains a Vortex of energy). We have traveled extensively throughout all four of its energy-calibrating doorways and retreated in the sanctuary of Gobean's luminous Blue Star. More about this as well as esoteric information is included in several chapters of this book.

I AM America has received a lot of publicity. But not everyone is a Vortex-seeker, and in the early 90s when the media came knocking on our door, they were primarily interested in the information surrounding the I AM America Map and its ancillary information about Earth Changes. We shared as best we could with what we understood. Then a novice to the I AM America teachings, I was only beginning to understand the spiritual depth of the information I was channeling. My evolutionary process provoked continuous inner questioning and a healthy, skeptical concern regarding the material. Was it accurate? What was the timeframe for Earth Changes? And this message was heavy—it was literally a doomsday scenario.

I prayed for strength and insight. Alongside the message of devastation and obvious destruction, the information held a polarity of hope and peace with the promise of an individual and collective spiritual evolution leading to a predestined global shift in humanity's consciousness. This seemed contrary and a bit confusing!

During a trip to Philadelphia, I found a dog-eared book on the Aramaic prayers of Jesus written in the 70s. The author delved into the topic of Prophecy and suggested that ancient Hebrew prophets never interpreted a single Prophecy in simple terms. Their viewpoint of prophecies revealed many subtleties and nuances through an arduous scrutiny, and this scholarly inquiry was threefold: literal, metaphoric, and mystical. Consequently, each Prophecy contained three messages. The first interpretation is verbatim—bare and unvarnished. This is the technique used primarily for the creation of the first I AM America Maps, as this was the only method we understood at the time. The second analysis is perhaps the most fascinating. This examination reveals inherent symbolism and allegories, and this valuable process redefines the Prophecy's tone and imagery. The final understanding distills the Prophecy into its most significant interpretation—a spiritual message.

This final progression lends cohesiveness to the development of the ability to discern and understand the intent of the Prophecy, which clearly is something different than prediction.

Naturally, this technique piqued my interest and after I applied this same method to the I AM America Earth Changes material, I came to the conclusion that the information I had received was not prediction at all—the information is indeed Prophecy. Cleverly hidden within the wisdom from the Spiritual Teachers is the esoteric insight to transmute every literal passage of destruction. Prophecy incites a personal and global healing process, something that lies far beyond prediction. And in order to heal, we must change physically, emotionally, and spiritually. I have included many articles that voice this new perspective on Earth Changes. In fact, this theme is supported throughout the entire book; simply stated, "A Change of Heart Can Change the World."

Since Prophecy is ideally a healing modality that prepares consciousness for change, many of the spiritual teachings in this book support this viewpoint. I think you'll enjoy the exploration on the Seven Rays and their movement from the Great Central Sun, the consciousness expanding Awakening Prayer, and the karma transmuting Violet Flame.

The critical information in this book is in fact about a new way of thinking and understanding. And this point cannot be over-emphasized. It may be our ability to grasp and apply this "new way" that literally saves us from a destructive psychology embedded in limited prediction-based thinking. This new way embraces a conscientious, holistic viewpoint of humanity; and our awakening consciousness extends onward to engender a new interaction with our sensitive environments—both social and physical, and throughout our precious Earth.

The Background

My first introduction to my Spiritual Teacher, Saint Germain, was through a third party, but eventually we did directly meet. I was twenty-two years old when I walked into a health food store in Sequim, Washington, and as I started to close the door behind me, the owner of the store pointed her finger directly at me and firmly stated, "You have work to do for Master Saint Germain!" I was an advertising representative at a small, weekly paper, and I had previously spoken on the phone with the store owner; she wanted to place an ad for a discount on strawberry jam. Twenty minutes ago her voice had been feminine, calm, and businesslike. The voice coming from the sales counter was definitely male, penetrating, and commanding!

I politely shut the door and approached the counter with some hesitation. "Who is Saint Germain?" I asked.

The storeowner responded in the same calm, kind voice that I recognized from our phone conversation: "Follow me. Back here." And she pointed to her office toward the back of the store.

I followed her through rows of neatly tiered vitamins to her office and noticed that on the wall was a picture of a man dressed in a powdered wig, waistcoat, and knickers, circa late 1700s. I felt an immediate recognition, like I had known him before. Logically, there was no way I could have ever met him, but the feeling was very intense. The storeowner held her hand out to me. "My name is Florence." Funny, I felt the same way about her too.

Florence went on to explain that Saint Germain was an Ascended Master and is a member of the Great White Brotherhood. These were all new terms for me and I asked her if she had any information that I could read. She gave me some printed literature and wrote down the names of several books. I had only been there a few minutes but it seemed as though time stood still.

That afternoon in 1978 changed my life; and Florence became a good friend and one of my first teachers of the Ascended Master tradition. Still, to this day I've wondered if the voice that predicted my work for my Spiritual Teacher was indeed channeled through her. And yes, I did pick up the ad for the strawberry jam!

CHAPTER ONE

Ascended Masters

What Is an Ascended Master?

An Ascended Master is a person who has gone through the human evolutionary process and has become liberated from the need to reincarnate in a physical body on Earth. Since Ascended Masters do not need to return to the Earth Plane, they are free from duality and the "Wheel of Karma." Their evolution continues in other dimensions, or lokas of experience. Often, they take on students (chelas) still learning in the physical plane and become their Master Teachers. Masters continue to have Master Teachers and their teachers also have teachers. Ascended Master Jesus, who is also known as Lord Sananda in his ascended state, and Kuan Yin, the Ascended Master and Bodhisattva of Compassion, are two of Master Saint Germain's teachers. This educational and spiritual lineage is the oldest on the planet and predates all of the world religions.

Hindu classifications of stages of spiritual advancement are documented in the Upanishads. They are: Siddha (perfected being); Jivanmukta (freed while living); Paramukta (Supremely Free—full power over death). Often, when an ascended being takes on a physical body to bring blessings to the world, he or she is known as an Avatar. The proof of this perfected free body is that it often casts no shadow or makes no footprints. Such Masters never appear in the gross public and have the power to become invisible. It is said that Saint Germain often takes the form of a beggar or old woman and is identified by wearing a piece of violet-purple clothing. Sananda once said that he is not limited by form of any kind, therefore he may take on any form or appearance necessary for the task at hand.

The Spiritual Hierarchy, sometimes referred to as The Great White (Light) Lodge, is a fraternity of men and women, composed of Ascended Masters and their students dedicated to the universal spiritual upliftment of humanity. Their chief desire is to preserve the lost teachings and spirit of the ancient religions and philosophies of the world. They are also pledged to protect against systematic assaults against individual and group freedoms that inhibit the growth of self-knowledge, development, and personal choice. And, most importantly, their mission is to re-awaken the dormant ethical and spiritual spark that has almost disappeared among the masses.

The Oral Tradition

Before electricity and television, the art of storytelling played a central role in relaying from one person or generation to another the traditions, values, history, culture, and heritage of native and indigenous peoples. But the true function of the oral tradition may be more than cultural preservation and artful entertainment.

According to the Master Teachers, before consciousness fell into the dark period of time that humanity is experiencing—what Indian scriptures call Kali Yuga—ancient societies and cultures lived and benefited from cyclic rounds of increased light frequency. Since the quality of light controls many life functions on Earth—including life spans, spiritual understanding, and mystical ability—the cycles of time explain the changing course of human evolution and development. The earlier cultures of Egypt and Atlantis suggest that humanity was at one time more evolved and readily enjoyed and employed the gifts of the super-senses, telepathy, clairvoyance, and clairaudience. There are many ancient Vedic texts that chronicle and describe human life and technology in other ages that is far superior and advanced when compared to our own.

Interestingly, before Earth's cyclic rotation around the Galactic Center ushered in the Age of Iron—Kali Yuga, humanity was given the gift of the alphabet. Since memory function would soon be substantially impaired during this era, the written characters of consonants and vowel sounds would provide a temporary house for images, important narratives, and legends that were once easily stored, organized, and cataloged for hundreds of years solely in the human mind. When we learn a spiritual concept or precept, set it to memory, and easily retrieve its contents through oral recitation, we are exercising and invoking a much higher and Divine Power than what simply reading about something will allow. The Master Teachers call this oral tradition of relaying information the function of "True Memory."

All of the I AM America trance-missions from the Master Teachers are given in the oral tradition. Through the use of this ancient tradition, parables and archetypes of consciousness are seamlessly relayed through the command of sound. The Kali Yuga language of the written alphabet is temporarily circumvented and a higher frequency emerges. This technique of ancient training, Master to student, guru to chela, is designed to open and develop subtle and latent powers currently dull and muted from lack of use. This important process and education is often described as the training of "the ears to hear."

CHAPTER TWO

Golden Age

The Four Ages of Time

According to Ascended Master teaching, our solar system receives light and is regulated by a greater sun—the Great Central Sun (a nonvisible quasar light). Ancient Vedic astrologers referred to this Sun as "The Galactic Center" and understood that our solar sun was in reality a double star with a companion dwarf star containing no real light of its own. As our solar system orbits the Great Central Sun, there are periods of time when the dwarf star blocks the inflowing light of the Galactic Center. Likewise, there are times when it does not. Since the light energy from the greater Sun nourishes spiritual and intellectual knowledge on Earth, the Vedic Rishis expertly tracked Earth's movement in and out of the flow and reception of cosmic light. This is known as the Cycle of the Yugas, or the World Ages, whose constant change instigates the advances and deterioration of cultures and civilizations. There are four Yugas:

The Golden Age (Satya or Krita Yuga);

The Silver Age (Treta Yuga);

The Bronze Age (Dwapara Yuga);

The Iron Age (Kali Yuga).

The Dharmic Bull of Truth symbolically represents this cyclic calendar. According to Vedic Tradition, the bull loses a leg, or twenty-five percent light, for each cycle of time. During a Golden Age, Earth receives 100 percent light spectrum from the great central Sun. In a Silver Age, 75 percent light, and in the Bronze Age, 50 percent light. We are now living in Kali Yuga (the age of materialism) and are receiving only 25 percent light.

(This material will be further explained in the section "The Kings of Kali Yuga.")

The Golden Age of Kali Yuga

As early as 1988, the Master Teachers often referred to the "Time of Transition"—a twelve-year period where humanity would experience tremendous growth in spirituality and knowledge that transforms personally and globally. This period was replaced in the year 2000 with the "Time of Testing," a seven- to twenty-year period where economies and societies would encounter instability and insecurities. These years will also mark a period of spiritual growth for humanity where brotherly love and compassion will play a key role in the development of Earth's civilizations as we globally move toward "The Age of Cooperation." During the Age of Cooperation, which is prophesied to last several thousand years, humanity will mark another New Age. The Master Teachers prophesy that these times will be recorded in history as one of Earth's Golden Ages.

Interestingly, other time systems concur with this Prophecy. Even though we are experiencing a darker time on Earth due to the influence of Kali Yuga (Kali Yuga's total reign lasts 432,000 years), some Vedic scholars see a glimmer of hope for humanity in the 10,000-year period known as the Golden Age within Kali Yuga. And we are experiencing this now.

Apparently, Kali Yuga began approximately 5,000 years ago. But according to the Bhavishya Purana, global changes and tribulations began around the year 2000 AD, alongside a continuous upswing in spiritual consciousness due to the influence of the Golden Age of Kali Yuga, which some say began around the year 1500 AD, others calculate that it began around 1898 AD. (The Bhavishya Purana is said to be one of the oldest and reliable Vedic scriptures on prediction; it accurately predicted the coming of Jesus, Muhammad, and Buddha.) This lesser cycle of light within a greater cycle of darkness will only last for 10,000 years and then the full effects of Kali Yuga (sans the Golden Age) will ensue. The Golden Age that we are now experiencing is considered to be a very important time for humanity's spiritual growth and evolution. Stephen Knapp, author of *The Vedic Prophecies*, writes, "During the period within the golden age of Kali Yuga, the spiritual opportunity for people increases, although we can plainly see that the standards for moral and spiritual principles also continue to decrease at the same time amongst most people, but not quite as rapidly. So it is a time that all people should try to take advantage of, because once it's over, you haven't seen anything yet." Clearly, this bright spot in an overall dismal cycle is given to "make hay, while the sun is shining."

Since the light of the central Sun, or Galactic Center, regulates the intelligence of humanity during the cycles of the Yugas, some Vedic authorities argue that mathematical calculations made during the darkness of Kali are inaccurate. This is the theory of Sri Yuteswar, disciple of Avatar Babaji and Paramahansa Yogananda's Master Teacher. He writes in *The Holy Science*, "The mistake crept into the almanac for the first time about 700 BC, during the reign of Parikshit, just after completion of the last Descending Dwapara Yuga . . . Together with all the wise men of his court, (he) retired to the Himalayan Mountains, the paradise of the world. Thus there were none in the court of Raja Parikshit who could understand the principle of correctly calculating the ages of the several Yugas." (It has been suggested that once the Rishis fled for refuge to the Himalayas, that they also took the sacred knowledge of Vastu Shastra—the Vedic science of Earth's geomancy—which later evolved into Chinese Feng Shui.)

Below is a table that reflects the timing of the Yugas, based on the work of Sri Yuteswar. Using this approach, in the year 2000 we have already experienced 300 years of a Bronze Age—Dwapara Yuga in the cycle of Ascension. It is also important to note that the Yuteswar Yuga Cycle (often referred to as the "Electric Cycle") is based on the movement of light through declining and ascending cycles. This descending cycle ceases at the lowest point and then begins an upward motion in the ascending cycle to the highest point of light. From a practical point of view, this would seem to make more sense than the commonly held viewpoint, prophesying a Golden Age directly following an age of Iron. This method reflects a more natural progression of light—i.e., spring, summer, fall, and winter, not winter directly to summer.

DESCENDING LIGHT	AGES	ASCENDING LIGHT
11,501 BC to 6701 BC	GOLDEN *(Krita)*	7699 AD to 12,499 AD
6701 BC to 3101 BC	SILVER *(Treta)*	4099 AD to 7699 AD
3101 BC to 701 BC	BRONZE *(Dwapara)*	1699 AD to 4099 AD
701 BC to 499 BC	IRON *(Kali)*	499 AD to 1699 AD

[DIAGRAM A: (Above) *The descending and ascending cycles of the Ages.*]

It is also important to understand that the Yuteswar Cycle uses a shorter cycle with just 24,000 years in one complete cycle. The traditional cycle contains 432,000 years, which begins in the year 3102 BC. So, which one is correct? Optimistically, the shorter cycle is a much more pleasant viewpoint, marking an obvious upward trend for humanity's growth and evolution. But it is entirely possible that we are experiencing two trends simultaneously—an overall downward phase containing a smaller, minor upward cycle as taught by Sri Yuteswar. Dr. David Frawley, Vedic authority and teacher of the ancient wisdom, addresses the issue: "I see humanity to be in a greater dark age phase, because even in the Golden and Silver Ages of the lesser cycle as evidenced in the Vedas, the great majority of human beings appear to remain on a materialistic or vital plane level, concerned mainly with the ordinary goals of family, wealth, and personal happiness. Only the higher portion of humanity, the cultural elite of a few percent, appears to experience the full benefits of the ages of light. This is the same as today, when the majority of human beings live on the same emotional level as before, and only a few really understand the secrets of science and technology, though all benefit from them."

If you overlay both systems, we are definitely experiencing an upward trend, major or minor, with the cycle of descending light beginning in the years 11,500 AD to 12,499 AD. Often the Master Teachers remind us, "The minutes and seconds tick . . . the Awakening is at hand. The time has come for man to receive the gift!" No doubt, we are living in an important time. And it is a time where we can begin, with the assistance of the upward cycle of Galactic Light, to evolve and develop through a finer harmonic. So why wait? "The time is now."

The Kings of Kali Yuga

"I beg to dream and differ from the hollow lies;
this is the dawning of the rest of our lives . . ."

~Green Day

It was 2008 and I'd received anti-Hillary email again. This message came from a friend, a Vietnam vet and avid Bush supporter who had soured due to the Iraq war. But he was not so sour that he'd support a Democrat for the Oval Office, let alone a woman.

"Well, who do you support?" I emailed in response.

I wasn't too surprised by his reply: "No one. There isn't anyone running I would vote for."

It seems today so many people who were once passionate activists for political and social reform have become apathetic. Have we become tired? Possibly. Or is it that we're older and wiser, and more carefully choose our fights? Perhaps the answer is as clear as my friend's email: we are living in a time where true leaders are few and far between.

I have no political affiliation, nor does the work of I AM America. However, I have observed the political arena with particular interest over the last fifteen years. Embedded throughout almost twenty years of I AM America information are fascinating prophecies of political and social change that are prophesied to happen alongside changes in weather patterns and global warming, creating an ultimate culmination of massive tectonic shifts. Some of the prophecies advised to watch the "political arena and presidential elections," to understand trends in collective consciousness and their relationship to Earth Changes. Many of these prophecies speak about the constitutional breakdown of our personal freedoms, the degradation of the office of the presidency, and the almost immobilization of our government, or even world governments to help to change this course. It's some dire stuff. In fact, at one time it was stated that we would "welcome the Earth Changes" over living in a future world allowed to continue in its present direction. All the options have seemed unacceptable, not to mention disturbing. Perhaps that is why indigenous cultures have often referred to this time as, "the Great Purification."

During the rough election year, we at I AM America continued to focus on the upside: Considering that these were prophecies, not predictions, couldn't we alter outcomes? Perhaps our own consciousness was the subtle link that could traverse this difficult transition. Alongside the potential for cataclysmic change, the information offered hope through the transformative restructuring of society and governments. The new paradigm would reflect our entry into a time of greater light and emergent evolution—a Golden Age.

As the nineties played out into the twenty-first century, our lives were far from golden. Housing prices had soared in many markets beyond reach; our president had been impeached by the House of Representatives and replaced by another who led our nation into war. We witnessed the terror of 9-11, the passing of the Patriot Act, and our country referred to as the "Homeland," for security's sake. I won't elaborate on the rising cost of healthcare, food, fuel, and energy.

A close friend phoned. Treating a cancerous tumor at a holistic center in Mexico, he fought tears as he expressed concerns about the future of the New Times. His life represented the reverse side of the spectrum: liberal, conscious, alternative. "I want it to happen now!" He pleaded. "I want to see a shift in consciousness."

Our lives are riddled with paradox. We are constantly assured that enlightenment is on the increase, yet so little demonstrates this as fact. Why does each hopeful glimmer of light seem to be matched by an opposing wave of darkness?

Over a dozen years ago I began the study of Jyotish—classic Vedic astrology, in an attempt to unravel answers. Jyotish, which means "the science of light," is based on the application of remedial measures—*upayes*—through light and sound. It is an ancient study, over 6,000 years old, of the art of prediction and how difficult life events can be mitigated through conscious awareness and diligent application. I have found this science enlightening and uplifting, but sometimes frightening. It can be uncannily accurate. One of my teachers said, "You must be strong to hear." This type of knowledge is not for sissies.

The end-times we are experiencing are correlated in Vedic prophecies as the Age of Kali Yuga, or the Age of Quarrel. Throughout the Srimad Bhagavatam, Vyasadeva, a renowned philosopher of Ancient India, prophesies that the leaders of this time—the Kings of Kali Yuga—are no longer, "Rajas." Raja means "One who shines." Leaders of Ancient India were required to possess this divine quality, alongside developed spiritual consciousness that could lead their people and society to hold love, compassion, cooperation, wisdom, and freedom as its foundation.

It is prophesied that the Kings of Kali Yuga would create wars to plunder and steal, and then hide like cowards leaving women and children as victims, shamefully neglected and without protection. Law and justice would evaporate as ideals and would instead be applied through the basis of power. The population of the Earth is prophesied to reach intolerable limits, where only the strong may gain power, and property is lost to merciless rulers who behave like ordinary thieves. Inhabitants are said to become emaciated by famine, natural disasters, wars, and taxation, while the political leaders "consume the citizens." The masses become increasingly ignorant regarding civics and government, and become unable to identify or vote for proper leaders. Remarkably these prophecies are thousands of years old, yet sadly echo a resounding truth for today.

In order to understand the age of Kali Yuga, one must first understand how the Ancient Rishis calculated time. According to their texts, our solar system rotates around a greater sun known as the Galactic Center (see The Four Ages of Time). As explained earlier, the Galactic Center is said to emit a type of non-visible light frequency—similar to a quasar—that controls spiritual evolution and growth on our planet. This light triangulates its energies to Earth through Mars, Jupiter, and primarily through our sun. The sun is said to be a double star, but its companion is a dwarf star, with no true luminosity or brilliance of its own. It travels alongside the sun, which may explain the irregularities in solar flares. This companion regulates the amount of galactic light which illumines Earth, and the measurement of this energy is indeed relational to each of the Yugas, or Ages of Time. During Krita Yuga (also known as Satya), which is a Golden Age, Earth receives 100 percent light from the Galactic Center; during Treta Yuga, a Silver Age, the Earth receives 75 percent light; during Dvapara Yuga, the Bronze Age, the Earth receives 50 percent light; and during Kali Yuga, the time we are currently experiencing, 25 percent light is received from the Galactic Center.

Since these light-energy spectrums control spiritual growth and evolutionary processes, they also regulate the level of intelligence on Earth, age spans, the ability to perceive and respect spiritual knowledge, and degeneration or advances in civilizations. There is also speculation that at critical junctures when the companion star alters its cycle from shadowing light (a descending cycle) to revealing light (an ascending cycle), or vice versa, a harmonization process with the new energies must occur on Earth. During these transitory periods of galactic light, many changes happen to the planet, nature kingdoms, and whole civilizations of humanity while adjusting to the new frequencies. This also creates potential for world cataclysm. Our collective ability to adjust or attune to this process can radically shift outcomes.

The Yugas are, at least from our earthly perspective, extremely long periods of time. In fact Kali Yuga[1], the shortest of the four, contains the least amount of years—432,000 to be exact—and to date, we have only experienced 5,108 of them! Since Kali Yuga is a cycle of descending light, this fact would seem a bit dismal if it weren't for yet another revealing Prophecy within the Vedic texts of the Brahmavaivarta Purana. Evidently Krishna prophesies a 10,000-year Golden Age that begins 5,000 years after the beginning of the Age of Kali Yuga. In essence, it is an age within an age, and Vedic scholars carefully describe this as the Golden Age of Kali Yuga. It is important to remember that this is not a full force 100 percent Galactic Light Krita Yuga, or Golden Age. This is a minor short cycle of ascending light within the larger descending influences of Kali Yuga. Since it is said that Kali Yuga began in 3102 BC, the beginning influences of the Golden Age of Kali Yuga started around the turn of the last century. I mention this Prophecy and possible timing as it gives confluence to the I AM America prophecies, and the birth of the Golden Age at this time. Currently we have experienced roughly 100 years of this smaller ascending cycle of light, only one percent of the total 10,000-year-long cycle. It also explains the overall downward and material influence of Kali Yuga on our governments, political leadership, technologies, cultures, and societies.

The apex of energy during the Golden Age of Kali Yuga is realized in the year 6899 AD. After that, light energies incrementally decline, when the 10,000-year cycle ends in 11,899 AD. Then the full effects of Kali Yuga ensue and there are many more prophecies in the Vedic texts that describe the declination of life throughout the remaining 417,000 years.

We may experience the effects of tyrannical leaders, changes in Earth's eco-systems, and witness devastating Earth Changes as we transit into a welcomed respite from the Age of Quarrel. The hope of a Golden

Age embedded within this time of trial and testing evokes optimistic possibility. It is an opportunity we should take full advantage of to uplift our world and, more importantly, ourselves. I won't sugar-coat it, however, and some suffering is likely to be endured as is the truth in any pivotal, transformational change. According to calculations, currently the Golden Age is at 1.09 percent . . . 1.09 percent and growing. (See Editor's Note below.)

Maybe there is a chance that in our lifetime, or that of our children or grandchildren, we may realize the foundation of the Rajas' remarkable kingdoms of peace and tolerance. Perhaps the legacy of the leaders of the world, the Kings of Kali Yuga, will be worth remembering, not lamented. The possibilities pivot on choice, and those choices, clearly, are ours. The potential for positive change is always engendered within, even though at times it may not seem that way.

Remember the Hopi Elder's Prophecy that circulated around the web several years ago? It starts, "You have been telling people this is the eleventh hour . . . do not look outside yourself for your leader . . . we are the ones we've been waiting for." I would suggest just one small change to this remarkable guidance: "We are the ones—the Rajas, the ones who shine—we've been waiting for."

[Editor's Note: In the *I AM America Golden City Series*, the Spiritual Teachers share information regarding how one may personally accelerate their energies beyond the current limitation of galactic light frequencies.]

Phrophecy is not a
    prediction

*Phrophecy is the letting go of
the unessential.

Prediction = declaration about
    future
phrophecy = addresses possibility
    + the potential for change
        – always gives a way out
    – shows us the drama to
    ignite change
        – it is a remarkable
    healing tool

CHAPTER THREE

Prophecies & More about Prophets

Prophecy Is Not Prediction

In Hindu culture, when a teacher wants to place the emphasis on an important point, the information is repeated three times. I imagine this is done so that the message is forever imbedded in the student's memory. With this intention, I'll make this statement: "Prophecy is not prediction. Prophecy is not prediction. Prophecy is not prediction." Now that we have that out of the way, you're probably asking, "Why?" Western culture does not and maybe has never understood the difference between Prophecy and prediction.

When examining Western culture from a spiritual perspective, one easily leaps to the conclusion that we are a material society. Just look at the array of smart-phones, luxury cars, and ATMs on every street corner. Our "toys" are our measure of success and comfort, and this value system can and does stop spiritual growth and evolution. But, it is not really our obsession with materiality that blocks the view. Rather, it is our mind. It is the way that we see things. The Masters call it "The Point of Perception."

Remember the iconic story of the three blind men hanging on to the elephant? Since each is in a different position, each defines the elephant according to the piece he's touching—different from the other two blind men. When we are dealing with something as dramatic and looming as Earth Changes Prophecy, we similarly see things according to whatever small piece we are hanging onto—which may be different from what another person perceives.

When people first encounter an I AM America Map, they either love it or hate it. Those who love it feel hopeful and happy that a New Time is coming. Those who hate it simply don't believe it, and sometimes point out that the map is geographically impossible. Over time, I have learned whether someone loves or hates the map, or thinks it is possible or impossible is not important. The map is a powerful metaphor of spiritual teachings, and therefore it releases the purifying, redemptive, and transformative experiential results of Prophecy—subtle yet extremely important.

Western culture's point of perception is extremely literal. We are over-identified with what we can only touch, see, smell, or hear, and unless we have scientific, empirical evidence, it doesn't exist. So why even deal with Prophecy? If "they" can't take it and make it into a date, a time, a correlation, a fact, a possible prediction, what good is it? But this thinking misses so much!

As I stated above, Prophecy is experiential. Throughout the years I've witnessed many people experiencing the tampering spiritual fires of Prophecy. Prophecy evokes fear and anxiety; the idea of losing anything we are attached to is horrifying. However, Native Americans encourage the process evoked by Prophecy—the letting go of the unessential—as purification. The visions and dreams of their prophets were the signals to do so and, through this process, their culture, their way of life, and their connectedness to Mother Earth were restored.

Eastern Indian Rishis heard the voice of the unconscious, and their position in their community as prophets and visionaries was considered invaluable. Once established on the spiritual path of listening to the inner-voice of wisdom, Prince Siddhartha, who later became known as the Buddha, denied an ego-voice that prodded him to: "Go back to the pleasures you have left behind." It was then that he declared that a philosophic "middle way" was the way one could be redeemed from illusion and experience unity. The Hopis say that humanity must "walk in balance," to prevent our world from experiencing calamity.

We westerners are fortunate to have one well-known body of spiritual teaching that could be classified as Prophecy: the Book of Revelations. When I was a little girl growing up in rural Idaho, we would listen to the radio every morning during breakfast. There was a program that came on before the news called *The Voice of Prophecy*. It was very evangelical and even my mother, who loves Christianity and is a devoted Lutheran, would roll her eyes when the show's song, which sounded much like a Sousa March and was sung by a barbershop Mitch Miller sort of trio, began, "Ring out the trumpet, and long live the King. Jesus

is coming again . . ." None of us ever believed it. In Sunday school, I
liked the idea that someday Heaven on Earth would come—but why
did we have to fight the battle of Armageddon to achieve this?

Today, through the help and example of our Native American
and Eastern Brothers and Sisters, I can see that Prophecy helps us to
address the spiritual battle that is often waged within ourselves through
the birth of our conscience and the redemptive power in our choice.
Prophecy is truly the balance that blends human fate with free will. This
occurs through Prophecy's physical, emotional, mental, and spiritual
prodding, that inevitably initiates a reevaluation of our current choices.
Again, the Master Teachers say that we have a choice how to react to
Prophecy—through whatever "Point of Perception" we choose.

And so Prophecy is not prediction. Prediction is a declaration about the future; Prophecy, however, addresses possibility and
the potential for change. One quick and easy way to tell the difference
between Prophecy and prediction is that Prophecy always gives a way
out, a solution so to speak, of what to do to avoid catastrophe. It's like
the option clause in a business contract that allows you to reconsider
a major purchase after twenty-four hours: the door that miraculously
opens in the eleventh hour; the inner voice that tells you to turn left
instead of right on your way home, thus avoiding a traffic accident. In a
Prophecy, the end result may be conveyed, not fated—if the urging and
prompting of Prophecy are heeded—and the results are transformative.

So don't get hung up on dates, earthquakes, shifting plates,
and volcanic explosions. That's just the drama of the story to get you
to change. The story is dramatic so that you won't forget it, so that it is
imbedded in your memory. Prophecy is not prediction! Get the point?

"*point of perception*"

Timing and Timelines

Timing and Prophecy is perhaps one of the most difficult aspects to understand. Because the prophesied events are possibility, not probability, the timing of these events is always ambiguous if they do indeed occur and are not simply lessened or ameliorated. Prophecy is an emotional word picture that is intended to astonish and surprise and even incite deep-seeded concern. This process rouses suppressed, unconscious fears that we may hold or not be aware of, and this spiritual route accedes to their recognition, transmutation, and inevitable release. Of course, along with this inner process, we begin to change the way we perceive our lives and the situations and circumstances that surround us. From this viewpoint, Prophecy is a remarkable healing tool.

The Spiritual Teachers do not relate at all to our perception of time! There may be several reasons for this. First, their outlook comes from a different dimension altogether, and when they speak or recognize our perception of "time"—which is nonlinear to them—"time" morphs into an *ever present now*. Many occasions we've asked, "When will the changes begin?" And they most always reply, "The time is now!"

Second, most Spiritual Teachers will rarely, if ever, interfere with our karma; so warning us about events that will happen in the next year or so is really not their intention. After years of working with their teachings, I have found that they often edify the universal, or natural laws, and will suggest how we can best apply them for our individual spiritual growth and enlightenment. Since Ascended Masters are free from the wheel of karmic retribution, they clearly understand our distinctive free will and the innate power of personal choice, and they rarely, if ever, will meddle. It seems we are here on Earth to learn through vital, personal experience which is fundamental to our evolution and empowerment.

In my early days of trance-work, they clarified their position on the use of dates for prophesied events, and at that time it obviously flew above our heads. But my recent re-examination of this material illuminates and explains their use of dates. They describe dates as "reference points." A reference point is a position in the landscape of time, the ever present now, where one can evaluate or weigh probability. Ideally, this point is positioned so we can initiate comparison between actual events, prophesied events, and then weigh the possibility of their timing.

The I AM America Teachings do not place an emphasis on the calculated time of prophesied events; rather, their possible transformation and change. With this in mind, the few dates that we've published in our materials were given to compare actual events to assess possible outcome. I have no doubt that when the Master Teachers first shared the I AM America Maps, they had grave concern regarding Earth's possible future into the 90s and the early 2000s. Fortunately, we are obviously doing much better. This might be due to the overall growth of lightworkers, the nonstop prayers and ceremonies for Earth and humanity enjoined by all faiths and denominations, and the growth of the golden light on Earth from the Galactic Center. I also think that because we engaged in purposeful yet arduous scrutiny of Earth Changes possibility throughout this entire time frame, we were able to shapeshift a different reality.

Clearly, it isn't over yet. Every week I update my Earth Changes blog with the most recent information on global warming and climate change, alongside earthquake and extreme weather events. Sadly, this aspect regarding the prophesied events is escalating, and the latest terminology regarding Arctic ice-melt is now scientifically recognized as, "Rapid Climate Transformation." Many years ago I interviewed with a newspaper in Atlanta, Georgia. The reporter was keen and responsive to the message of Earth Changes Prophecy and asked me this question, "So if I understand you correctly, we should never disregard Prophecy; it is a spiritual teaching?" I whole-heartedly agreed and reminded her that it was almost impossible to update a Prophecy or alter the impact that its story may have on the consciousness of the listener. I smiled when I received a copy of her article, it was titled, "The Perpetual Warning."

phrophecy is a healing tool

. mk ultrs
. mountoulk project

stillness in thestorm website

(yellow cube)

Spiritual Insights on Earth Changes

1. Since our planet and humans share the same physical composition, we are virtually ONE. You cannot disconnect the two.

2. Our world is a thought, feeling, and action hologram created by many kingdoms, (mineral, vegetable, animal, human, etc.), that inhabit Earth. The Earth and our bodies have many systems—these systems are interrelated.

3. Every individual thought, desire, and action is recorded, and subsequently influences and creates a "Collective Consciousness."

4. Collective Consciousness plays a major role in the outcome of events. It can make the difference between a cataclysmic hurricane and a gentle summer rain.

5. If you live fear, you will create fear.

6. If you live love, you will create love.

7. We are all creating and experiencing World Earth Changes as an opportunity to develop personal Mastery and evolve spiritually.

8. We must change ourselves enough that this change reflects in our societies, governments, and environments. We have a conscious choice in the upcoming Earth Changes, and that choice will help determine the outcome.

9. This is an urgent time—the time is now!

"what you take with you is what you see"

Prophecies of Political and Social Change from the I AM America Material

In the New Times there will be several political centers in the United States. (See chapter 4.) Of significance will be the five Golden City regions of the United States and five different regional (state-like) governments will evolve. One significant political capital will emerge in Colorado, currently near Crestone, Colorado (often referred to as the "Crystone").

The Five Golden City Vortices of the United States are:

1. Gobean: Arizona and New Mexico; Qualities: Transformation, Harmony, and Peace
2. Malton: Illinois and Indiana; Qualities: Fruition (fructification), Attainment
3. Wahanee: Georgia and South Carolina; Qualities: Justice, Liberty, and Freedom
4. Shalahah: Montana and Idaho; Qualities: Abundance, Prosperity, Healing
5. Klehma: Colorado, Kansas, Nebraska; Qualities: Continuity, Balance, and Harmony

Prophecies:

1. Five Stars will represent the new nation, after the Earth Changes.
2. During the Earth Changes, our nation's capital and political center will be moved to the Golden City of Klehma (in Colorado). This will also become the new location for the re-establishment of a monetary system.
3. Before the major Earth Changes escalate, there will be severe economic crisis and hardship throughout the world.
4. The Masters' prophesy that after the Times of Changes, a bartering system will be established. They recommend that investments should be made in tradable resources, e.g., gold, silver, land, and other natural resources and commodities.
5. Until the new US monetary system is established, economies will function on a regional basis. Gold and silver will be used, but in its older forms—nothing new will be minted.

6. Our new monetary system will be based on transportation. The ability to travel to the Golden City Vortices will be highly valued.

7. A True State Economy will evolve. This is an economy based solely on trading with precious metals, natural resources, and goods. Because this type of economy is based upon what it produces, printed money or fiat-currencies are prohibited. This model closely resembles a Natural Economy, in which money is not used to transfer goods and resources among people.

8. Throughout the world, governments of republics and open societies will emerge and evolve.

9. Republic: A government of elected representatives. A republic is also defined as a government that is headed by an elected or nominated president, not a hereditary leader. A key feature of a Republic is the presence of the Rule of Law, which requires that the government reflects the self-interest of the people subjected to the law. Governments must act in the national interest, alongside the right of self-determination.

10. Open Society: The concepts of the Open Society were the original philosophies of Henri Bergson, who advocated that governments be responsive and tolerant, and above all, transparent and flexible. An Open Society keeps no secrets from the public, and political freedom and human rights fundamentally lie at its foundation. Leadership is changed without the need for revolution, coup d'état, or bloodshed, which often defines the closed societies of monarchs and dictatorships. A well-known example of an Open Society is Democracy.

11. There will be many changes in the human body and its energy centers (chakras) and system. According to the Master Teachers, the changes on the Earth will affect human DNA coding at the molecular level. This change prepares the human body for the New Dimensions.

12. The Master Teachers have always taught that one of the signs that the Times of Changes are nearing is a high rate and escalation of crime. Saint Germain says, "When insanity becomes sane, the Times of Changes will be coming."

13. Time Compaction: An anomaly produced as we enter into the prophesied Times of Changes. Our perception of time

seems to compress—moving extremely fast—with many events compressed into a short period of time. This experience of time will become more prevalent as we get closer to the period of cataclysmic Earth Changes.

14. Cosmic Wave Motion: Cosmic wave motion is explained as belts of energy that exist in the universe, similar to an oceanic tidal system. This movement is prophesied to originate from the sun moving to a certain point in the Universe, and then reversing. This reverse motion encounters other forward moving waves, and soon forward and reverse moving energy waves weave an infinite pattern covering the Universe. According to the I AM America Prophecies, the movement of the waves and their influences on planets control time and subsequently evolution. During the Times of Changes on Earth, the "jumbling and tumbling" of cosmic wave belts causes time to go very slowly, or causes it to speed up into time compaction. The planets Saturn and Neptune are prophesied to help adjust the waves as they impact Earth, affecting humanity. This wave motion is at first disruptive to animal and human nervous systems. The waves also trigger an evolution in consciousness, and initiate greater understanding of unity and compassion.

15. The time period or duration of the Times of Changes may be as short as six years, and may be as long as 1,000 years.

16. The cleansing and purification of the Earth is also a purification of many various systems. This purification or process of transformation occurs at many levels, outwardly and within. The systems that are prophesied to undergo tremendous changes are:

a. The Deva Kingdom
b. The Elemental Kingdom
c. Nature Spirits
d. The Vegetable and Flower Kingdom
e. The Mineral Kingdom
f. The Animal Kingdom
g. The inner-self of every person on Earth

17. New Age of Utopia: These are the ideals for a perfect society, as outlined by the prophecies:
    a. Lasting and committed marriages
    b. Stable family life
    c. Economies are inflation free
    d. Organic Agricultural systems
    e. Charity—not welfare
    f. End of useless taxation
    g. No crime
    h. No police force
    i. Open Libraries and Schools
    j. Use of many languages
    k. Holistic healthcare
    l. No nuclear threat
    m. Interaction with Nature Kingdoms

18. During the Time of Change, the Earth's energies will change and transform. Areas (like Vortices) will open that will be known as "Transportation Centers." Through utilizing the Earth's unique energies, these areas will allow us to travel to nonphysical dimensions and back again. Several of these areas prophesied are near Coeur d'Alene, Idaho; another near Bismarck, North Dakota.

19. New agricultural areas will be developed in the North Dakota area, and later near Albuquerque, New Mexico.

20. After the changes, advanced technology will be applied to control the weather through crystal devices. This technology will be utilized to stabilize the weather throughout the west coast of the United States, which will have suffered the most drastic of Earth Changes.

Prophecies of Peace:

A series of spiritual laws and teachings designed to lead humanity and the Earth into a New Time of enlightened thinking and harmonious living.

1. After the Times of Changes we will experience a time of Peace on Earth.

2. We are moving beyond the Third Dimension in conscious experience, and onward to Fourth and Fifth Dimensional understanding.

3. The human Chakra System is changing alongside the energy systems of Mother Earth.

4. The New Times will bring many changes in our governments and societal structures.

5. The family unit will change significantly in the New Times, and children are conceived and birthed in a different way. The higher spiritual energies produce children conceived first through thought and higher consciousness.

6. Many life streams are coming to Earth who do not have as high a karmic burden as those of the past. These new souls raise the consciousness of the Earth and are blessed with Dharma.

7. A portion of the new souls that incarnate on Earth are known as the Seventh Manu. These special children are conceived and sponsored through the process of conscious thought. Others are born in the Golden City Vortices. They play a tremendous role in raising the overall Vibration of the Earth.

Spiritual Prophecies:

1. During and after the Time of Change, a new cultural paradigm will evolve. This new paradigm is based on healing, transformation, abundance, harmony, and peace for all people.

2. During and after the Times of Changes many people will ascend into the higher dimensions and planes of consciousness. There will be many geo-physical (sacred) places on the Earth during this time that will assist this physical and spiritual process.

3. The Earth Changes are a way to usher in a new way of thinking and being.

4. Since the shape of the Golden City Vortices is based on sacred geometry, their shape is also affiliated with the Polar Shift. The polar shift is approximately a 45-degree angle. This physical shift also represents a massive shift among humanity toward spiritual consciousness.

5. Age of Peace: An age of time when humanity is prophesied to experience the New Age of Utopia. During this time, the Vibration of the Earth and humanity will be raised, and there will be no cataclysmic Earth Changes. The message of Peace is demonstrated first in our hearts. It is then shared with our families, and extended into our daily affairs and throughout our communities.

6. The Birth of the Feminine or Soletata: (Pronounced So-lee'-tah-tah) the conscious expression of the Divine Feminine. The divine feminine as taught in this context is not feminism, but rather, a celebration of all that is feminine. It provides support and service to the masculine energies, and gives conception and birth to all on Earth, including the Nature Kingdoms. It is identified as nurturing, with an open heart and hearth. In Master Teachings, Soletata is a Divine Spiritual Energy that unites the Christ energies within (child and mother), and recognizes father as "Divine Spark." It is cultivated through simplicity and the natural domestic activities of nurturing and caring for children, baking bread, growing gardens, and hanging laundry in the wind. In esoteric Taoist traditions, when properly united with masculine energies, the feminine opens the door for profound spiritual development and internal alchemy. Physically, this can open energy channels, or meridians of the body, allowing a subtle harmony that integrates the body and promotes healing.

7. Many souls will choose to not experience the upcoming changes, and will leave the planet before the Earth Changes begin. They will do so by insanity, involvement in addictions, disease.

8. Unana (Unity Consciousness) is prophesied to exist among the masses: The path leading to this state or level of consciousness starts through the simple Mastery of thoughts, feelings, and actions. The union of these three energy bodies—the mental, emotional, and physical—produces the alchemical marriage of

the masculine and feminine forces in the body. According to Master Saint Germain, "This initiates Unity Consciousness." However, it is added that individuality, or the undivided state, comes first. Proceeding is the next natural state, contact with the ONE. This higher form of consciousness is all-knowing, all-pervading, and all-powerful. In this state of existence, all is connected as one larger, nonphysical, yet thinking and feeling, body. "Unana," (pronounced ooh-nah'-na) is the name the Ascended Masters have given to this level of inter-connectedness, where the mind moves beyond individuality and into a unified field of consciousness.

9. Ascended Masters will be assisting the Earth to avert the most cataclysmic Earth Changes. We can assist this effort through our positive thoughts, prayer, and meditation.

mental + emotional + physical = masculine feminine

Prophecies for the I AM America Map

Canada, United States, Mexico, Central America, and South America—known by the Spiritual Teachers as the "I AM America Map."

[Editor's Note: The following pages contain many "literal" Earth Changes Prophecies. To learn their metaphoric and mystical interpretation, see *Freedom Star Booklet*.]

Canada and Alaska

In Alaska, the North Slope melts due to rising seas and global warming. Alaska will also be hit by several tsunamis. Overall, the climate gets warmer in Alaska. When the ice melts, there will be remnants of ancient civilizations that underwent massive Earth Changes in the past.

The western coastline of Canada will change. In the future, this change will allow for better transportation routes to Alaska.

The Canadian territories of the Northwest Territories and Nunavut, and the two Canadian islands of Victoria Island and Baffin Island are prophesied to break into many islands. The western coast of the Canadian province of British Columbia is prophesied to sink, and the Rocky Mountains define its new coastline following the present-day Coast Mountains. Southern Alaska and the city Juneau are also prophesied to sink in this Earth Change. The Kenai Peninsula meets a similar fate; however, the Alaskan city of Anchorage remains. The Aleutian Islands are prophesied to disappear into the Pacific Ocean. The Yukon Territory loses land on its northern coastline due to global warming. A new bay forms in Alaska and the Yukon Territory and floods the Yukon Flats, leaving the Alaskan town of Fairbanks a seaport town in the New Times. The Province of Alberta remains unscathed during the Earth Changes.

The Saint Lawrence River and gulf are prophesied to widen significantly during the Time of Change leaving the cities of Ottawa, Montréal, and Quebec under water. It is also prophesied that Northern Quebec (Ungava Peninsula) breaks into small islands. Labrador becomes an island. Newfoundland has few changes; however, global warming raises ocean waters, leaving many of its southeast coastal land and towns under water. For more information on Canada and Alaska, see *New World Wisdom, Volume One*. (Formerly *New World Atlas*).

Greenland

During the Time of Change and due to global warming, it is prophesied that Earth's oceans will contain little or no fish; however, the oceans near Greenland will retain remnants of this precious sea life. The lands of Greenland are prophesied to thaw, sizably reducing the island's size and coastlines.

United States

Every state in the United States will be affected by the changes. The first events start in the year 1992 and will continue for hundreds of years. During 1992, these events took place:

A 6.8 earthquake in eastern Turkey killed 500 people.

One of the most destructive hurricanes ever, Hurricane Andrew, raged through the Bahamas, Florida, and Louisiana.

Hurricane Iniki struck the State of Hawaii, Kauai and Oahu.

1992 Tornado Outbreak: November 21–23, eastern and midwestern US. This outbreak was the largest and longest on record.

All of the four elements will be involved during the changes: fire, water, earth, and air.

Prior to a mega-quake in Oregon, Earth is bombarded by a massive shower of meteorites. These numerous impacts cause an ash cloud to envelope Earth's atmosphere, and tremendous rainfall. We experience massive flooding all over the world. Rivers, seas, and oceans swell.

The increased water causes increased pressure on fault lines. This leads to massive earthquakes and mega-quakes.

After the strike of an asteroid, there will be many earthquakes in California. This will lead to massive earth movements that inevitably leave most of California under the Pacific Ocean. The Sierra-Nevada Mountains will become islands, and one large island containing the Lake Tahoe area, Yosemite Park, and Sequoia National Park will be formed. A peninsula of land will extend out to Mount Shasta extending near Crater Lake, Oregon. This peninsula later erodes into a series of islands. Surrounding the largest island that is fashioned from the changes in California—Gibraltar Island—are many smaller islands. These are called "The Pathway Islands" They are very stable geo-physically and will exist for hundreds of years. These islands exist to the north between

Gibraltar Island and the Mount Shasta peninsula. The Baja Peninsula slowly erodes into a series of islands which will be known as the "Diamond Islands."

In the Pacific Northwest, ash from exploding volcanoes will hide the sun for two years. Seattle will be covered by water. A new coastline in the Pacific Northwest covers most of the current state of Washington. This is due to a series of earthquakes and mega-quakes that occur throughout Washington and Oregon. Much of Oregon sinks due to a massive earthquake. The new coastline extends west to La Grande, Oregon, where the Wallowa Mountains become a new chain of islands. The Cascade Range of mountains becomes islands. Mt. Baker and Mt. Rainier become islands. During the changes, Oregon becomes engulfed by the Pacific Ocean. This happens in several stages: first, the ocean laps into the Willamette Valley; then the ocean moves east, beyond the Cascade Range; the Wallowa Mountains become the new coastline near La Grande, Oregon. The Blue Mountains and the Wallowa Mountains become chains of islands.

The new Continental Divide of the United States starts near Livingston, Montana, as a new range of mountains, known as The Cooperation Mountains.

The Bay of Harmony, which is formed by the Pacific Ocean covering much of California, Nevada, and the northwestern and western portions of Arizona, is a very shallow bay. It is almost impossible to navigate. The beaches are very gradual and the water is not deep, limiting the ships and boats in this bay. However, the waters of the Bay of Harmony create coastline cities of Phoenix and Sedona, Arizona.

From the Bay of Harmony, a river passage opens to Denver, Colorado. Denver's proximity to this river passage and the new ocean coastline help it to prosper as a seaport city in the New Times. A new ocean bay will be formed west of Denver, Colorado. Denver will not be affected much by the Earth Changes; however it will feel tremendous earthquakes. Most of Utah will eventually be under water. The range of mountains—the Wasatch Range—becomes a series of islands that will be renamed "The Tablet Islands."

The lands in eastern Montana as well as North and South Dakota experience very few changes. A new Continental Divide forms. Starting in central Canada, this range of mountains follows the flow of the River of Cooperation (new Mississippi River), extends into Kansas, as far south to present New Mexico. At the beginning of the mouth of the River of Cooperation, it is almost two miles wide. The Missouri and Mississippi Rivers eventually merge and become one large river, known as the "River of Cooperation."

The Mississippi and Missouri Rivers flood. The Mississippi River will almost cut the nation in two. The Mississippi River forms a large bay covering large portions of Texas. Houston and Corpus Christi are under ocean waters. The newly widened banks of the Mississippi River cause the river to be named "The River of Cooperation." Because this becomes one of the major sources of fresh water in the nation, this large river becomes a major source of irrigation water in the United States. Areas along the River of Cooperation become the new agricultural areas of the nation. Most of the state of Louisiana becomes a salt-water bay. Baton Rouge is under water, along with New Orleans. Eventually a small island appears near Lafayette, Louisiana, becoming a delta area.

Lake Michigan drains near Chicago, Illinois, further creating a bay in Texas. Lake Michigan drains, and the remaining Great Lakes change and form one large lake—Unity Lake. Chicago will experience tremendous flooding during the changes, due to the drainage of Lake Michigan, but it will survive the changes.

On the east coast of the United States, there will be high winds. Northern portions of Maine will be covered by ice. During the changes, Washington, D.C., will experience strong, cold, frigid winds. A large energy Vortex currently covers New York City, extending into Connecticut, New Jersey, and Pennsylvania. During the Times of Changes, the energy of this Vortex—not a Golden City Vortex—becomes "misplaced." (During the changes many Vortices and lei lines move and shift, along with "Earth Changes." However, this word from the trance-scripts indicates a misuse of energy. Could it be a nuclear disaster?) This causes a constant wind to blow throughout this area, which will become covered by water, and nothing will live there for some time after the major Earth Changes. Also, no islands will form. This bay will be named, "Reconciliation Bay."

After the changes, Washington, D.C., will cease to be the capital and political center for the United States. However, for many centuries into the New Times, the symbols that are contained there (i.e., Washington Monument, the Capitol Building, etc.) will be preserved.

In the future, many will travel to view the symbols and their historical significance.

In Maine and parts of New England, because of constant thawing and freezing, much of the land erodes. The land and the climate become unstable. There will be an earthquake in either Lake Erie or Lake Ontario. This massive quake will inevitably lead to the sinking of land around Washington, D. C.

The east coast of the United States does not have major earthquakes; however, much of the land breaks up into small islands due to flooding and high winds. In the New Times, the east coast will be peppered with many small islands.

Due to global warming and climate change, the United States will experience the "see-sawing" of the four seasons. Winter can become summer, and spring can immediately become fall. Hurricanes and tornadoes will become common weather anomalies during the Time of Change. For more prophecies and information about Earth Changes Prophecies in the United States see: *I AM America Map, 6-Map Scenario, Freedom Star Map,* and *Freedom Star Booklet.*

Mexico, Central America, and South America

Massive earthquakes are prophesied to break Mexico's Baja Peninsula into a series of islands. These same earth movements are prophesied to ripple the entire west coast of South America, causing enormous earth slides of coastal lands into the Pacific Ocean and submerging the Yucatan Peninsula. Several hundred years later, movements of tectonic plates form the Cooperation Mountains. This new range of mountains is prophesied to exist from the United States, through Central America, and extend into South America. Another mountain range is prophesied to rise during the Time of Change, comprising the Yucatan Peninsula, the West Indies, Cuba, Puerto Rico, and the Virgin Islands. This mountainous chain—the Silver Crystal Mountains—will connect Cuba and Venezuela and enclose the Caribbean Sea. The ocean waters of the Caribbean Sea are prophesied to become one of the world's largest fresh-water seas in the future, and it is surrounded on all sides by this new ring of mountains. Much of the west coast of South America is prophesied to change through volcanic, earthquake, and tsunami activity. Most of Chile is underwater, and Bolivia and Argentina comprise the new western coastline. Lima, Peru, becomes a coastline city. The lands of Patagonia and Argentina become a free-floating island as the southern tip of South America breaks into islands, with a larger island forming to the north of the Falkland Islands.

The Amazon River basin widens into a large bay, and Colombia has both a west coast that touches the Pacific Ocean and a small east coast, where the waters of the Atlantic Ocean lap. A large bay forms near Rio de Janeiro; however, several small islands form near this Brazilian city, known as the Islands of Southern Brazil.

Prophecies for the Greening Map

Japan, Korea, China, Australia, and India are known by the Spiritual Teachers as "The Greening Map."

A large peninsula of land rises in the Sea of Okhotsk, and Sapporo, Japan, is located on its most southern coastline. This greatly reduces the size of the Kamchatka Peninsula, on both sides—to the west and the present-day Sea of Okhotsk, and to the east is the Bering Sea. Due to planetary global warming, most of northern Russia is under water and breaks up into islands and peninsulas. The Stanovoy Mountain Range forms part of the new northern coastline in Russia and China. Beijing, China, is underwater.

Japan breaks into three smaller islands and suffers many tsunamis and earthquakes. Osaka and Tokyo are under the Pacific Ocean. Both North and South Korea break into islands; however, the Golden City of Presching manifests over North Korea—which is a Golden City of the Angels (see chapter 4).

Bangladesh and lands that border Bhutan and Nepal flood and eventually create a large bay—the Bay of Scented Flowers. Kanpur, India, is located on the coastline of this new bay. Ocean waters cover the Great Indian Desert. Pakistan is also deluged, and India now resembles a free-floating island, with a singular umbilical peninsula connecting it to mainland Asia. Delhi and New Delhi are located on this unique peninsula of land.

The Himalayan Mountains rise to even higher elevations in the New Times.

A large river, almost like an ocean bay, forms in the center of India, between the Western Ghats and the Eastern Ghats. This becomes a sacred river for India, and its waters flow from the north, near the Golden City of Prana, to the south, and empty into the ocean. Bangalore becomes a coastal city on the west side of this large, river-like bay. Large earth rifts open central China, forming the Great China Peninsula. Wuhan, China, is located on the northeast side of this large peninsula, and Chengdu, China, is under the waters of a new ocean bay to the west of this peninsula. Lanzhou, China, becomes a seaport city. The waters of what will be known as "The Blazing Bay" will cover Hanoi and most of Laos, including Da Nang. A large ridge of new mountains rises in the center of Laos and extends into China; this is known as "The Rim of Eternal Balance." Most of Thailand and Cambodia, which are to the west of this new chain of mountains, are underwater in the New Times, and parts of southern Myanmar (Burma) are also prophesied to be under the present-day Bay of Bengal.

Australia breaks into two halves, and Alice Springs becomes a seaport city. New lands rise in the Coral Reef and in the Coral Sea and connect to the eastern half of Australia. The central and southeastern coastlines of Australia remain unscathed during the Time of Change, however Melbourne and Adelaide suffer many changes and are nearly covered with the ocean waters with many tsunamis. Tasmania Island pivots to the northeast in a severe shift of tectonic plates. Hobart becomes the center of the new island.

This same tectonic shift literally reveals a new continent, prophesied to appear near New Zealand, and these new lands are four times the size of this present-day southwestern Pacific Ocean country.

[Editor's Note: For further study regarding the prophesied physical Earth Changes see *Freedom Star World Map*.]

The Map of Exchanges: Europe and Africa

The Earth Changes Prophecies for Europe and Africa are perhaps the most alarming. As the Earth Changes close in the islands of Japan, Europe chimes in with riddling earthquakes and volcanic explosions, and the dawn of the new world is near.

In the prophecies, harmony is born as the perception of separation dissolves. As Earth accepts Fourth-Dimensional consciousness, alignment shifts the layers of the atmosphere and great tears occur in the first three layers of the atmosphere. The phenomenon of ice sheeting occurs, as huge layers of ice (some as large as one mile thick) cover areas throughout Europe and Western Asia; some regions are ten square miles in diameter.

Europe and Africa develop into conscious lands of spiritual exchange, and a bridge of conscious collective thought extends a creative wave onward to reach the cosmos. Through this expansion and assimilation, the Earth and humanity receive Rays of universal healing. It is prophesied that two of the most focused Ascended Masters of healing assist: Lady Nada, Europe; Master Kuthumi, Africa.

The first event for Europe is prophesied to begin roughly after the sinking of the upper portion of Vancouver Island (Canada). The original reference point was around the year 2000—so this timeline has morphed into the future. Tectonic plates in the Atlantic Ocean grind, and a series of earthquakes strike northern Europe. Especially affected are Norway, Sweden, Finland, and Eastern Europe, with this earth movement felt far east into Moscow, Russia. Soon, torrential rains and windstorms are prophesied to hit the coast of England, France, and Spain. During the second shift of the pole, lands in England, France, and Germany are engulfed by the newly formed Ocean of Balance. Cities engulfed in this Earth Change are: Helsinki, Stockholm, Oslo, Copenhagen, London, Dublin, Hamburg, Berlin, Warsaw, Krakow, Amsterdam, Brussels, Paris, and Bordeaux.

Global warming shifts ice and glaciers. Combined with rising waters and erosion, the breakup of land forms many new islands in upper Ukraine, Sweden, Germany, and France. These cities become New Age seaports for the Ocean of Balance: Glasgow, Sherffield, Manchester, Essen, Prague, Berdichev, and Galati.

The lands of Iceland rise, with the Reykjanes Ridge raising in a tail-like shape on the southwestern portion of the island.

Tears in the ozone layer create sheets of ice crashing onto Eastern Europe and remaining parts of Poland and Germany. The thermohaline current of the Atlantic Ocean changes direction and temperature. This occurs for several years.

The next event for the Map of Exchanges is the formation of the Sea of Grace. This corresponds to the rising of the Himalayan Mountains into the Awakening Mountains. As this massive Earth Change occurs, the Black Sea, the Azov Sea, the Caspian Sea, and the Aral Sea all form one large body of water—the Sea of Grace. Lands lost in this Earth Change are: sections of northern Turkey, parts of Iran and Afghanistan, Ukraine, eastern coastlines of Romania and Bulgaria and extending north to the Ural Mountains. Newly created seaport cities are: Zonguldak, Tehran (approximately 100 miles from the new coastline), Samarkan, Turkestan, Baikonur.

The Ural Mountains form into a large island, named the Shiny Pearl. This island becomes a trade center for the Ocean of Balance with seaport cities covering her coastline. Several of these present-day cities are: Kuybyshev, Ockenburg, Aktobe, and Sterlitamak. During the Earth Changes, many people will migrate to this island and it evolves into one of the most prosperous lands in the New Times.

At the close of the period of worldwide cataclysmic Earth Changes, many scientific experiments evolve into a major nuclear detonation. Through this manmade change, (which enlarges the Mediterranean and Red Seas), the Sea of Eternal Change is born. Her waters cover the lands of Libya, Egypt, Sudan, Israel, Jordan, and western Syria, the western coastline of Saudi Arabia, northern Ethiopia, and Tunisia. Much of Italy, Yugoslavia, Albania, all of Greece, and southern Turkey are covered by ocean waters. Cities lost in this change are: Rome, Venice, Naples, Barj, Tirane, Athens, Izmir, Thessaloniki, Tripoli, Tunis, Benghazi, Alexandria, Cairo, Yafo, Beirut, Tel Aviv, and Jerusalem. New Age seaports for the Sea of Eternal Change are: Ghat, Omdurman, Khartoum, Addis Ababa, and Asmera. On the eastern coast of the Sea of Change: Mecca, Medina, and Tobruk. More cities surrounding this new sea: Damascus, Aleppo, Sofia, Milan, and Turin.

Within the next twenty to thirty years, the Persian Gulf, (now renamed Bay of Holy Prayer), widens through more shifting of tectonic plates, forming another large bay into the Glory (Indian) Ocean. Lands lost are the western coastlines of Oman, Saudi Arabia, and Iraq. New

Age coastline cities are: Riyadh and An Najaf. The Euphrates and Tigris River basin is covered with this new sea and the western coastline of Iran is buffered by the Zagros Mountains.

The final land movements for the Map of Exchanges begin when new lands enlarge the countries of Portugal and Spain. This original reference point was around 2100 AD, but is likely hundreds of years into the future. Lands enlarge the southern tip of Africa and the countries of Namibia and South Africa, and the Island of Madagascar doubles in size. With this movement, the western coastline of Africa falls into the Atlantic Ocean, creating new coastlines in the countries of Algeria, Morocco, submerging all of Western Sahara, Mauritania, and Senegal. A new coastal bay, the Bay of Protection, enlarges the Gulf of Guinea, cutting into central Africa's Nigeria and Cameroon. Central African Republic and the country of Chad now have coastlines on the Atlantic Ocean.

The southern coastlines of the African countries of Guinea, Ivory Coast, and Ghana drop into the Atlantic Ocean/Guinea Basin. The countries of Sierra Leone and Liberia are submerged in this Earth Change as well as most of Togo. Gone are the cities of Freetown, Monrovia, Abidjan, Accra, Lome, Porto Novo, Lagos, and Bioka. A 400-mile swath cuts into the western coast of southern Congo and Angola, sinking all of Cabinda.

The eastern coastline of Africa breaks into a series of tiny islands, creating a large coastal bay near Lake Victoria and the Rift Valley. This Earth Change destroys all of Somalia and Ethiopia becomes a seaport country to Glory Ocean. Kenya, Tanzania, and Zimbabwe also touch Glory's waters, and Mozambique is broken into many small islands.

South Africa splits apart and the inland country of Botswana becomes a seaport country. Cities gone in this Earth Change event are: Muqdisho, Dar es Salaam, Maputo, and Durban.

After these changes, more Earth Changes ensue for over 200 years and new lands emerge. The rising of the ancient lands of Lemuria complete Earth's entry into the millennium of peace and grace. The first new lands of Lemuria are seen northwest of the Hawaiian Islands, around the 30° latitude and 170° longitude. Another large continent reveals itself that enlarges the lands of New Zealand from approximately the 55° latitude south to the 5° latitude. This new continent, larger than

Australia, also includes the Fiji and Samoan Islands. The birth of this new land appears with the rising of the Tonga and Kermadec Ridge and the Austral Seamount Chain.

As the ice caps melt in global warming, new lands are revealed at the South Pole. The final earth movement begins hundreds of years into the Earth Changes and new lands form a peninsula on the South Pole region with the raising of the Scotia Ridge.

[Editor's Note: Read this endnote for a quick understanding on the evolution of the idea of cataclysmic change in geology and the "Law of Uniformity." [2]]

A Genuine Prophet—Always Wrong!

By now you are likely in shock, disbelief, or completely overwhelmed after reading these literal prophecies. Please indulge me for a minute. Closely examine your "feeling" and allow that emotion to move you internally into metaphoric thinking. Now, re-consider the information. At this stage everyone is a bit different. Some rapidly flow into the images of Prophecy and their inherent allegories, while others do not.

As mentioned earlier, when Westerners hear the words "prophet" or "Prophecy," their likely response will be, "Oh yeah, Armageddon." And since the Book of Revelations is the only significant body of Prophecy that the Western world has yet to experience, this inclination makes perfect sense. Traditional cultures of the East are often referred to as "descending cultures" that protect customs and beliefs based on literally thousands of years of individual practice and knowledge. Through this time-worn, ancestral wisdom, descending cultures innately understand the heart of Prophecy and know that this spiritual teaching is an important signal to personally purify and seek redemption and healing.

The Master Teachers present the I AM America Prophecies to illustrate how individual balance and harmony are created through our daily choices.

The common difficulty and subsequent confusion of Westerners who confront Prophecy is due to the fact that their ears are not trained to hear metaphor. This makes the truest comprehension of the meaning of Prophecy—written in the language of the super-conscious—almost impossible. Joseph Campbell said, "The Metaphor is the Mask of God through which eternity is experienced." The spiritual teachings that are conveyed by most prophecies are designed to open your ears to a richer understanding of meaning.

Traditional biblical Armageddon destroys the old world, rewarding the gift of paradise to the deserving: again, another age-old battle arguing the ethics of good and evil. But the path of Prophecy is experiential. The visions of Prophecy are spiritual teachings containing warnings which—if experienced and heeded—are designed to heal and renew our experience of our lives.

So please don't call our office and ask, "When is this going to happen?" Honestly, we don't know.

We can only share the messages with you and leave it up to you to interpret. However, we might point you to the Twelve Jurisdictions

(Spiritual Teachings that are given in *New World Wisdom*). Or address the Golden Cities and how Earth and Human energy fields are ideally ONE.

There is a saying that a prophet's work is truly complete when the events that are prophesied never occur. If they do not occur, then those who had the "eyes to see" and the "ears to hear" made the choice to heal and transform their lives. Catastrophe and destruction may be averted or avoided altogether. So inevitably, a genuine prophet always has egg on her face.

[Editor's Note: The sequence for understanding Prophecy is threefold through literal, metaphoric, and mystical interpretation. Metaphoric thinking bridges our consciousness to experience and realize the healing energy of Prophecy at a holistic and enlightened level.]

The Time of Testing

Remember Y2K? Everyone was concerned that, across the globe, all computers would crash and we would face an inevitable technological Armageddon. We at I AM America received a fascinating message around that timeframe, and the teachings focused on the topic "The Time of Testing." This is a twenty-year period (2000 to 2020) and prior to this twenty-year period, we experienced a time period often referred to as "The Time of Transition."

"The Time of Transition" was a twelve-year period (1988 to 2000) when the Beloved Ascended Masters, Archangels, and Elohim flooded the Earth with Light (the Rays) to increase and subsequently evolve our individual spiritual growth. Many people have known and understood this period in humanity's history as "The Spiritual Awakening." This twelve-year period was very important in the Spiritual Hierarchy's plan to increase true spiritual awareness among humanity and to demonstrate the "Law of Love in action." During this twelve-year period, many of us witnessed the growth of alternative self-help and healing groups and increased interest in alternative forms of spirituality from Native American shamanism to Tibetan Buddhism. Truly, we are united as ONE consciousness and ONE human heart.

Alongside the growth of a United Brotherhood and Sisterhood, Mother Earth began a purification process. Global Warming was the greatest concern with flooding in the Midwest of the United States. Also evidenced in President Bill Clinton's 1994 State of the Union address:

> "When the earth shook and fires raged in California, when I saw the Mississippi deluge the farmlands of the Midwest in a 500-year flood, when the century's bitterest cold swept from North Dakota to Newport News, it seemed as though the world itself was coming apart at the seams."[3]

There were devastating floods in other areas of the world: Central America and in Venezuela. Terrible earthquakes in Japan, Algeria, Turkey, and Taiwan, alongside climatic changes producing incredible windstorms in Europe, typhoons in India, freak tornadoes in the United States from Utah to Texas and into Georgia. We also saw freakish winters on the East Coast alongside terrible hurricanes leaving thousands homeless.

These were the events that we expected. Edgar Cayce said it would happen sooner, Nostradamus wove the prophetic events into his quatrains and Hopi Prophets simply uttered, "The Great Purification." The Spiritual Hierarchy continued to reinforce the teachings of personal choice, the mainstay instruction during "The Time of Transition" and our ability to alleviate, decrease, and possibly circumvent cataclysmic Earth Changes altogether through a change in our collective hearts and minds.

In "The Time of Testing," the Master Teachers say the opportunity for our spiritual growth and worldwide peace has never been more apparent. Earth Changes events will continue to escalate alongside our spiritual growth and opportunities to learn and Master the lessons in love, harmony, and cooperation. We'll have all of the necessary education to lay the foundation for the New Times—The Golden Age! "The Time of Testing" is a period when humanity will understand the nature and the power of personal choice. A wise friend once said, "You are never tested beyond your capability." Master Saint Germain also reminded us that "making a plan" is very important. Here are a few tips:

1. Make a list of your top six goals.

2. Create an outline of action steps for each goal.

3. Take the realistic actions for each step to achieve your goals. See your outline as a road-map of your future. This outline is very personal and sacred. Place it in a special place in your home (on your personal altar, etc.) and use decrees and meditation to assist its outcome.

1. Help inspire as many people as possible
2. Personal spiritual development
3. Change the direction of generation
4.

On the Other Hand . . . The Law of Opposites

Two distinct opinions have developed around Earth Changes. The first is that Earth Changes are not necessary, and with the proper attitude and actions, devastation will be circumvented and an ensuing Age of Peace and Prosperity for the Earth and her peoples will reign. The second opinion sees the necessity of Earth Changes to cleanse and purify the Earth and humanity's current state of self destruction. In both scenarios, balance is the desired outcome.

Everything in creation is based upon the Law of Opposites. All things appear in twos—known in many spiritual traditions as duality. Duality is seen everywhere: literally, metaphorically, and mystically. For instance: Rich/Poor; Fear/Courage; Light/Dark. The examples are endless. Even our own body is divided into male and female, the left side is female and the right is male.

Creation is visible and invisible, and all dimensions, planes, and levels of awareness are subject to the Law of Opposites. However, it is important to understand that all manifestations are dual expressions of the ONE. The ONE is important to understand in order to comprehend how all interpretations of Earth Changes Prophecies have their place in the motion that exists through the Law of Opposites. It is also important to understand that while certain prophecies may oppose one another, they eventually come together and create balance.

Visualize this: a simple playground teeter-totter. (See Diagram B.) On one side is male, (yang), and on the other side is female, (yin). The center is the fulcrum, or in this case, the ONE. The ONE is the source of the teeter-totter between male and female. It is the source of the interchange between the two opposing forces and always stays the same.

You'll note that with each movement, male or female change position in the interchange of energy. One is up, or one is down. You'll also notice that in the interchange of energy, all things are forever changing into their opposites. This is a natural law and rules all created things. This cycle of change rules seasons and weather. It rules plants and animals, it rules the Earth in its motion around the sun, and it rules you and me. This law of eternal change is also known as the Law of Balance.

Law of eternal change = Law of balance

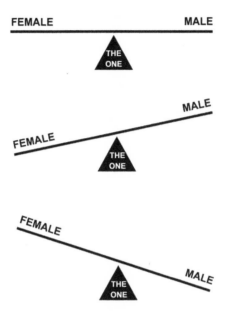

[DIAGRAM B: (Above) *An illustration depicting the "Law of Opposites."*]

See how the teeter-totter works? Every movement one side makes, the other side must answer; yet, there is always the changeless point: the fulcrum; the changeless; the timeless ONE. It is the source of the movement, and yet it never moves! Since it never changes, the Spiritual Teachers claim it is the only thing that is real. It is the point of perfect balance and contains both sides.

Flow! grid

Earth Changes: Free Will and Predestination

During many years of explaining and teaching the I AM America Map of Earth Changes prophecies, we would hold up a map and ask people, "What do you see?" We did this as a Rorschach test—encouraging viewers to see the images as symbols that might reveal their subconscious beliefs and concerns. Of course, many eagerly raised their hands and declared, "I see Earth Changes!" But every now and then, there was the one who would say, "The Golden Age."

It is true. The I AM America Map contains both scenarios. Devastating climatic change, earthquakes, erupting volcanoes, destruction beyond our present experiences—Earth Changes; and also a vision of a New Time, graced with spiritual experience and beauty beyond our comprehension—the Golden Age. Each yellow area on the I AM America Map represents a sacred place to the Ascended Masters. They proclaimed in the earliest descriptions, "Gateways, or Vortex areas, are protected areas for interaction with Spiritual Energy." We continue to learn much more about the Golden City Vortices in our discourses from the Master Teachers. Some of the basic information is that there are fifty-one such cities throughout the entire world. Again, the five United States Golden Cities are:

1. Gobean (pronounced Go'-be-an) located in Arizona and New Mexico.

2. Malton (pronounced Mal-tone') located in Illinois and Indiana.

3. Wahanee (pronounced Whah-haw'-knee) located in South Carolina and Georgia.

4. Shalahah (pronounced Shaw-law'-hah) located in Montana and Idaho.

5. Klehma (pronounced Clay'-maw) located in Colorado, Kansas, and Wyoming.

Golden City Vortices have individual, unique energies. Each city's energy identifies with a Ray Force and a specific Master Teacher. These unique energy anomalies will mature throughout our entry into the New Times and they contain many healing forces that work on all levels: physical, emotional, mental, and spiritual.

While many have focused on Golden Cities Vortices as safe places during cataclysmic Earth Changes, we receive reports on a daily basis from those who have traveled to the huge Vortices to experience their power. Many report increased psychic awareness, lucid dreaming, connection with Spirit Guides, a high-pitch hum, and, of course, healing at many levels. Dowsers have reported phenomenal energy irregularities throughout their massive span, most likely identifying further energy points and sub-Vortices.

But the most definitive and clear communication contained in the little yellow areas of the I AM America Map is the message of hope. The energies in these cities reflect a most unique spiritual understanding of duality; predestination versus free will. Is it the end of an old age or the birth of a New Time? Will we experience the worse, simultaneously with the best? The answers to these questions are again up to you. How do YOU see the picture?

James Braha, in the book *How to Be a Great Astrologer*, addresses the same provocative question: "There is no darkness without the possibility of light. One is not a mother without a child. Likewise, there is no free will without predestiny. The two are dependent upon each other."

CHAPTER FOUR

Golden Cities

What Exactly Is a Golden City Vortex?

Golden City Vortices—based on the Ascended Masters' I AM America material—are prophesied areas of safety and spiritual energies during the Times of Changes. Covering an expanse of land and air space, these sacred energy sites span more than 400 kilometers (270 miles) in diameter, with a vertical height of 400 kilometers (250 miles). More importantly, Golden City Vortices reach beyond terrestrial significance and into the ethereal realm. This system of safe harbors acts as a group or universal mind within our galaxy, connecting information seamlessly and instantly with other beings. The Master Teachers call this phenomenon the Galactic Web.

As mentioned earlier, fifty-one Golden City Vortices are stationed throughout the world, and each carries a different meaning, a combination of Ray Forces, and a Divine Purpose. Some are older than others; some Vortices are new; and some shift locations. The activation of Golden City Vortices occurs in patterns—that's the crux of the numbering system. The Master Teachers call Earth "Beloved Babajeran."

Although the Masters, as a group, oversee all Golden Cities, each Master stewards his or her own Vortex. A Golden City Vortex works on the principles of electromagnetism and geology. Vortices tend to appear near fault lines, possibly serving as conduits of inner-earth movement to terra firma. The Gobean Vortex near the fissure-filled Mogollon Rim of Arizona; the Malton Vortex of the Midwest, adjacent to the New Madrid fault line; and the Shalahah Vortex of Idaho, an ancient cleft near the Snake River and Hells Canyon, lend credibility to this theory.

Geology has a profound effect on the potency of a Vortex. Not surprising, the five Golden City Vortices rest on areas of highly magnetic geologic formations. The iron-rich content of basalt pillars and ancient-lava deposit serve as natural conductors of electromagnetic energy; igneous rocks, according to geologic data, create more magnetic pull than sedimentary rocks. That's why Gobean exudes so much energy. Landmarks—such as Mount Baldy in Arizona, the apex of the Southwestern Vortex, and the Golden City Vortex of Shalahah—are filled with basalt and iron-rich rocks.

Water also drives the disbursement of Vortex energies. The Gobean Vortex sits atop the largest aquifer in the Southwest. Shalahah, too, surrounded by three, huge freshwater lakes near Coeur d'Alene and Pend'Oreille, Idaho, and Flathead Lake in Montana draws power from water.

Visitors to Golden Cities experience spiritual and psychic development—they feel a heightened sense of balance, harmony, and peace. The Golden Cites are natural places of meditation, connection with spirit guides, and contact with past-life experiences. Vortices can instantly align the human energy field (aura). During your first stay in a Vortex, you may sleep more while your body adjusts to powerful energies. As you acclimate, you'll undergo a rejuvenation of the body and the spirit. After the shock subsides, many Vortex-seeking pilgrims will engage in prayer and group ceremonies with friends and spiritual mentors, awakening deep connections among fellow humans.

[Editor's Note: For more information on the Golden Cities and their exact locations in the United States, see the *I AM America United States Golden Cities Map*. To view the worldwide network of Golden City Vortices, see the *Freedom Star World Map*.]

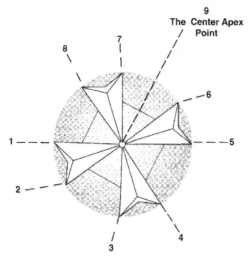

[DIAGRAM C: (Above) *A Golden City Vortex, and its first nine points.*}

Vortex Symbology and Sacred Numerology

The visual shapes of the Vortices are a series of symbolic pyramids. The pyramid is the spiritual symbol of the descent and ascent of Divine Energy. The first shape is built on nine points, (nine the number of Divine Man), and the second shape defines dimension (See Diagram D), adding four more points, (four is the number of the Earth representing her four elements: earth, air, fire, and water). The first nine points represent the descent of Divine Power into the world. By adding four points you achieve the number 13. Thirteen is the number of transformation and rebirth, (e.g., Twelve Apostles and the Christ; Twelve signs of the zodiac and the sun), thirteen also symbolizes leaving anything binding you and it moves you into a new creation. This structure completes with the nine, and thirteen points sharing one continuous point, the apex. In the prophecies, the apex is the most powerful and significant location in the Vortex. The sacred numerology leaves fourteen points, total, that reduce to the number 5. Five is known as the number of freedom and intelligent communication.

Additional insights on the number five, are given by Manly P. Hall: "The pentad—5—is the union of an odd and an even number (3 and 2). Among the Greeks, the pentagram was a sacred symbol of light,

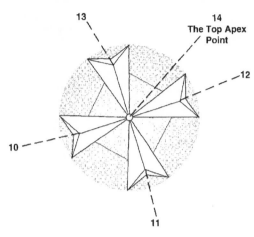

13

14
**The Top Apex
Point**

12

10

11

[DIAGRAM D: (Above) *A Golden City Vortex, the last five points.*}

health, and vitality. It also symbolized the fifth element—ether—because it is free from the disturbances of the four lower elements. It is
called equilibrium, because it divides the perfect number 10 into two
equal parts.

The pentad is symbolic of Nature, for when multiplied by itself,
it returns into itself, just as grains of wheat, starting in the form of seed,
pass through Nature's processes and reproduce the seed of the wheat
as the ultimate form of their own growth. Other numbers multiplied
by themselves produce other numbers, but only 5 and 6 multiplied by
themselves represent and retain their original number as the last figure
in their products.

The pentad represents all the superior and inferior beings. It is
sometimes referred to as the hierophant, or the priest of the Mysteries,
because of its connection with the spiritual ethers, by means of which
mystic development is attained. Keywords of the pentad are reconciliation, alternation, marriage, immortality, cordiality, providence and
sound." [4]

The significance of the number five is easy to remember. Hold
up your hand and count your four fingers, joined by one thumb. The
simplicity of our hands reminds us that we are four elements, (four
fingers), joined by the fifth element, (the thumb), spirit. Manly Hall
expands this concept: "The tetrad (the elements) plus the monad (one)
equals the pentad. The Pythagoreans taught that the elements of earth,

fire, air, and water were permeated by a substance called ether—the basis of vitality and life. Therefore, they chose the five-pointed star, or pentagram, as the symbol of vitality, health, and interpenetration."

Elements
Fire
Water
Air
Earth
Ether - #5

tetrad + monad = pentad
(four)   (one)   (five)
(elements) (spirit)
                  pentagram is sacred
                  symbol of light

Pyramids and Vortices

The pyramids in Egypt represented to this ancient culture a new beginning and the pyramid-shaped hillock was used extensively in their agricultural practices. Each spring, the flooding Nile would recede and carefully cultivated hillocks would emerge, rich and fertile, ready for planting. Each small shaped hillock was symbolic of the reborn world.

Pyramids were also built, not as observatories or tombs, but as temples. The Great Pyramid was associated with Hermes, known as the Divine Illuminator, and worshipped through the planet, Mercury. (Mercury is also associated with the number 17.) The pyramid temples were erected as physical displays of secret truths which are the foundation of all arts and sciences. "The twelve signs of the zodiac, like the Governors of the lower worlds, are symbolized by the twelve lines of the four triangles," writes Manly Hall, "The three main chambers of the Pyramid are related to the heart, the brain, and the generative system—the spiritual centers of the human constitution. The triangular form of the Pyramid also is similar to the posture assumed by the body during the ancient meditative exercises. The Mysteries taught that the divine energies from the gods descended upon the top of the Pyramid, which was likened to an inverted tree with its branches below and its roots at the apex. From this inverted tree, the divine wisdom is disseminated by streaming down the diverging sides and radiating throughout the world."

[handwritten notes in margin: "why? inverted"]

[handwritten note at bottom of page:]
Greek — mathmatical language of harmony
Owaspee — native language of the angels

Golden City Names

The names of the Golden Cities are unusual, and each city's meaning is secret knowledge closely held by the Master Teachers. Through the years of our work with the Ascended Masters, several definitions of the names of Golden Cities have emerged, but never in great detail. Yet, each curious name is important and reveals hidden qualities and spiritual characteristics of each Golden City. Some occultists refer to the veiled language of the mystics as Owaspee—the native tongue of Angels. The Divine Language, or the language of the Gods, is referred to in religious traditions including the Adamic language—the language spoken by Adam and Eve; Hebrew—the Jewish language of God; Greek, the mathematical language of harmony; and Sanskrit, the Divine Language of the Gods through Vedic spiritual traditions.

Divine Languages are often known as form languages. My Vedic teacher once explained the etymology of Sanskrit as "a Mother tongue," similar to the syntax and semantics of computer languages. According to Vedic legend, our entire Earth was programmed, or created, through the spoken words of Sanskrit. Speaking a form language is powerful and commanding, and each spoken syllable has the ability to exactly create in form and substance its subject. Perhaps the creation story of Genesis says it best: "Then God said, 'Let there be light,' and there was light." (Genesis 1:3 New American Standard Bible)

The names and meanings of the Golden Cities, which originate in the Causal Plane of the Fifth Dimension, carry their emotive light and sound through the feeling worlds of the Fourth Dimension and integrate their activity to evolve the HU-man—the spiritually enlightened, realized God-man—of Earth's Third Dimension. Golden City names are founded in the multiple languages of Earth. Their individual syllables are based on archetypal words from many cultures of the world, including ancient Sanskrit, Greek, Persian, Phoenician, and the lost tongue of Moriori. Their sounds also include Native American languages: Algonquian, Navajo, Shoshoni, and Cahto. Surprisingly, modern languages appear in the syllables of the names of Golden Cities: the universal language of peace, Esperanto; J. R. R. Tolkein's fictional language of Middle Earth, Elfish; and the contemporary, linguistic Minimalist Language.

The sounds and meanings of the Golden Cities' names are both the evocations and myths for the New Times. Their resonance is the hope and the aspiration for progressive, positive change on behalf of humanity and Earth. The theosophist George William Russell wrote, "The mind of man is made in the image of Deity, and the elements of speech are related to the powers in his mind and through it to the being of the Oversoul. These true roots of language are few, alphabet and roots being identical."[5]

Alphabet = roots

Meanings of the Fifty-One Golden City Vortices

ADJATAL: *The Big Rainbow* derives its meaning from the Suabo-Indonesian word *adja* ("big") and the Pashto-Pakistanian word *tal* ("rainbow"). The Golden City of Adjatal is located in Pakistan, Afghanistan, and India; the historical Khyber Pass (the ancient Silk Road) is located on the western side of this Vortex city.

AFROM: This Golden City name means, "A Devotion." This meaning originates with the word *from*, which in German, Norwegian, and Swedish means "pious" or "devoted." The Ascended Masters claim this Golden City also means "to affirm."

AMERIGO: This European Golden City is Spanish for "I AM Race."

ANDEO: The Golden City of the South American Andes is likely named for this mountain range; however, the source of this Golden City of the Feminine is rooted in the Albanian word *anda*, which means "strong desire," and the Huli (New Guinea) word *andia*, which means "mother." Andeo's meaning translates into this phrase: "the Mother of Desire."

ANGELICA: The Native American Algonquian word *ca* means "at present" or "present"; therefore, Angelica's full meaning is "Angel Present," or "Angels at Present."

ARKANA: The nineteenth-century language of peace—Esperanto, and the Polish language both state that the word *arkana* means "Mystery."

ASONEA: The Golden City of Cuba and ancient Atlantis derives its meaning from the pristine Ason River of the Cantabria province in Spain and its mythological race of supernatural undines—the *Xanas*.

BRAHAM: *Braham* is also known as the Second of Three Sisters who preserves a maternal radiance over South America. Braham is the feminine version of *Brahma*, and this Golden City meaning is the "Mother of the New Manu."

BRAUN: The Golden City of Germany, Poland, and Czechoslovakia means "the Shining Strong One."

CLAYJE: Dialects from the Netherlands create this Golden City's name through the word *kla*—"clear." The word *je* in Bosnian, Croatian, Serbian, and Slovak languages means "is." The combination of these words constructs this Australian Golden City's meaning: "Is Clear."

WOW

CRESTA: In Spanish, Italian, and Brazilian Portuguese the word *cresta* means "the ridge or peak."

CROTESE: Located in the Cradleland of Central America, this Golden City means "the Attentive Cradle." Its meaning is derived from the French *cro*—"cradle," and the Etruscan *tes*—"to care for or pay attention."

DENASHA: This Golden City derives its meaning from the modern English name Denesa, which means the "Mountain of Zeus." This mythological Greek father of both Gods and men is also known in Roman myths as Jupiter, an ideal symbol for this European Golden City of the Yellow Ray.

DONJAKEY: Located on new lands prophesied to rise from the Pacific Ocean in the New Times, this Golden City's name comes from the Italian word *don*—"gift," and the Indonesian word *key*—"tree." Donjakey means "Gift of Trees," and is associated with new species of flora prophesied to appear on Earth.

EABRA: "The Feminine in Eternal Balance." This name is a derivative of several words, namely *bra* or *bodice*, which means "the pair" or the "wearing of pairs." *Ea* has several meanings: in Frisian (German) *ea* means "ever," in Romanian *ea* means "she." The word *pair* numerically indicates two, a number associated with femininity and balance.

FRON: The meaning of this Australian Golden City is "throne" in Albanian. In the Creole language, *fron* means "pious" and "devoted." The combination of these definitions creates Fron's meaning: "the Devoted Throne."

GANAKRA: The ancient Turkish City of Ankara means "anchor" in Greek; in Portuguese *gana* means "desire"; and *kra* is a Creole word for "mind." Ganakra's combined meaning is "Desires Anchored by the Mind," or "Desires of the Mind."

GANDAWAN: From the Sanskrit word *Gondwanaland* means "Forest of the Gonds." Located over the Sahara Desert, this Golden City represents this ancient culture that claimed to survive in present-day India. Contemporary Gond legends mirror the emergence stories of Southwest Native American tribes, and the Gond Gods surfaced from a cave and were adopted by the Hindu Goddess Parvati (Divine Mother) and were assisted by their tribal Goddess Jangu Bai. According to myth, the Gonds emerged from their cave in four distinct groups.

GOBEAN: The Ascended Masters claim Earth's first Golden City for the New Times means to "go beyond." However, Gobean's etymology suggests the meaning: "Go Pray." This phrase is derived from the word *bea* or *be*, which in Frisian (German) and Norwegian means "prayer."

Arizona & New Mexico

GOBI: Named for the Great Desert of China, Gobi in Mongolian means "the waterless place." Ascended Masters claim the Golden City of Gobi is a step-down transformer for the energies of Earth's first Golden City—Shamballa. Gobi's esoteric definition comes from the Chinese translation of "go—across," and *bi* in Indonesian (Abun, A Nden, and Yimbun dialects) means "star." The Golden City of Gobi means "Across the Star," or "Across the Freedom Star." "Freedom Star" is a reference to Earth in her enlightened state.) Gobi aligns energies to the first Golden City of the New Times: Gobean.

GREIN: *Grein* is an Icelandic, Norwegian, and Swedish word which means "branch." The Ascended Masters maintain that the New Zealand Golden City of Grein means "the Green Branch"—a symbol of the peaceful olive branch.

GRUECHA: The Golden City name of Norway and Sweden is a Norwegian word and means "Hearth."

HUE: According to the Ascended Masters, the word *hue* invokes the Sacred Fire, the Violet Flame. In Tibetan dialects, however, the word *hue* or *hu* means "breath."

JEAFRAY: The Golden City of the Ever Present Violet Flame meaning translates to "Yesterday's Brother." This is based on the Gaelic word *jea*, which means "yesterday"; the word *fra* is English for "Brother" (friar). Since Archangel Zadkiel and the Archeia Amethyst serve in this Vortex retreat, "Yesterday's Brother" is a reference to the work of Saint Germain—as Sanctus Germanus (the Holy Brother)—and the many other archetypes of consciousness who tirelessly work for humanity's freedom and Ascension through the use of the transmuting fire.

JEHOA: It may be that this Golden City's name is based upon the Tetragrammaton YHWH; however, the etymology of this sacred haven of the Caribbean is based on the Russian word *YA*—meaning "I AM"—and *hoa*, which means "friend," from the Tahitian, Hawaiian, Maori, and Rapa Nui (Easter Island) languages. This translation elevates the various interpretations of Jehovah, the jealous God, into the uplifting phrase, "I AM Friend."

KANTAN: This Golden City of China and Russia derives its name from the English (Cornish) word *kan*—which means "song," and the Korean word *tan*, meaning "sweet." The full meaning of this spiritual Vortex is the "Sweet Song."

KLEHMA: The meaning of the fifth Golden City of the United States is based on several Native American words. The first syllable *kle* (pronounced clay) comes from the Navajo word *klê-kai*—which means "white." The second syllable *ma*, is a derivative of the Shoshoni word *mahoi*—around, or encircling. Klehma's esoteric definition is the "Circle of White." *Colorado, Kansas, Wyoming*

KRESHE: This African Golden City is known to the Ascended Masters as the "Silent Star," an esoteric reference to Venus. *Kres* is also a Celtic word for "peace."

LARAITO: This Ethiopian Golden City's meaning is "Our Home." Laraito's definition comes from the Brazilian, Portuguese, and Spanish word for home—*lar*. *Ito* is a Tanzanian word for "ours."

MALTON: The Ascended Master Kuthumi's Golden City meaning is derived from the Phoenician word *maleth*—which means "a haven."

Illinois & Indiana

MARNERO: Mexico's Golden City's steward is Mother Mary and the first syllable of Marnero—*mar*—is a Spanish, Italian, and Portuguese word which means "sea" or "ocean." The remainder of the name—*nero*—translates into *ner,* a Hebrew word for "candle." The Golden City of Marnero's meaning is the "Ocean of Candles."

MESOTAMP: The Golden City of Turkey, Iran, and Iraq is likely linked to the ancient word *Mesopotamia*, which means the "land between rivers." The higher meaning of *Mesotamp*, however, is linked to the New Guinea word *meso*—"moon," and the Turkmen word, *tam*—"house." Mesotamp's meaning translates into the "House of the Moon."

MOUSEE: This Golden City for the New Times means the "Ocean of Fish." This spiritual haven, prophesied to appear near Hawaii, combines the New Guinea word *mou*—"fish," and the Afrikaan word *see*—"sea" or "ocean." New flora and fauna is prophesied to appear as Earth enters the New Times.

NOMAKING: This Chinese Golden City means "Name of the King." Its meaning is based on the word *noma* (or *nama*) and in many languages ranging from Italian to Sanskrit simply means "name."

PASHACINO: "The Passionate Spirit." This Canadian Golden City's meaning is derived from the English word for "passion"—*pash*, and the Kurdish and Turkish word for "spirit"—*cin*.

PEARLANU: Madagascar's Golden City's meaning is based on the Malagasy (the national language of Madagascar) word *lanosina*, which means "to be swum in." Pearlanu's meaning translates to "Swimming in Pearls."

PRANA: Located in the heart of India, this Golden City of the Pink Ray meaning is "Life-giving Energy."

PRESCHING: This Chinese Golden City's meaning is linked to its topography. *Pres* is an English word which means "meadow," and *ching* is a Native American (Cahto) word for "timber and forest." Presching means the "City of Meadows, Grasslands, and Forests."

PURENSK: This Golden City means "Pure Intelligence" or the "Pure Message." This Russian and Chinese Golden City derives its esoteric meaning from the Danish, English, German, and French name *pur*— "pure," and the Turkish word, *esk*, for "intelligence" or "message."

SHALAHAH: Sananda is the steward of this United States Golden City which in Sanskrit means a "Sacred Place Indeed!" The syllables break down with these meanings: *shala*—"sacred place", "sanctuary"; *hah*— "indeed." *[handwritten: hahas (11)?]* *[handwritten: Montana & Idaho]*

SHEHEZ: This Golden City located in Iran and Afghanistan is a Persian word that means "large," or "grand."

SHEAHAH: The Ascended Masters claim that the meaning of this Australian Golden City is, "I AM as ONE." The etymology of this Vortex meaning is undoubtedly related to the Feminine Energies prophesied to dominate and direct the New Times. The syllable *aha* in Tanzanian and Uganda means "here"; in Czechoslovakian *aha* stands for "I see." Therefore Sheahah's hidden meaning is actually prophetic: "She is here," or "She, I see."

SIRCALWE: The Russian Golden City of the White Ray derives its sacred name from the Turkish and Chinese languages—*sir*, which means "secret"; and the Elfish language of Middle Earth—*cal*, meaning "light." The word *we* in the English, Korean, and Italian language is defined as "ours." These languages combine to give this Golden City Vortex name its meaning: "Our Secret Light."

STIENTA: This Golden City's name means "the path" in Norwegian.

TEHEKOA: Since this Golden City represents one of the Three Sister Golden Cities of South America, its meaning springs from the lost Moriori language and the Hebrew word *Teku'a*: "the City of Tents," "secures the tents." These meanings merge and Tehekoa means the "Wise Woman who Secures the City."

UNTE: This Golden City—located in Tanzania and Kenya—means in Brazilian, Spanish, and Portuguese "to anoint."

UVERNO: The Canadian Golden City of the Pink Ray translates in Slovak to "trust well."

when (II) ?

WAHANEE: The third Golden City of the United States derives its name from *Wahabu*, the Nigerian name for the "God of Love." The etymological meaning of the final syllable *nee* in English, Italian, and French is "born." Wahanee's esoteric meaning is the "God of Love is born."

SC/6A

YUTHOR: In minimalist language, *Yu* means "union." *Thor* is the Scandinavian God of Thunder—"Power." The Golden City of Greenland's hidden meaning is the "Power of Union."

ZASKAR: This Golden City of the White Ray derives its meaning from the Czech and Slovak word *zas*—"again," "over again"; and the Basque word *kar*, which means "flame." This Chinese Golden City means the "Repeating Flame."

[Editor's Note: The *Webster's Online Dictionary with Multilingual Thesaurus Translation* was used extensively in creating this translation. For the exact locations of the Golden Cities see *Freedom Star Map* and *Freedom Star Booklet*.]

Golden Cities of Other Times

In the last 2,000-year period, the planet held a Golden City Grid consciousness through thirty-three Golden City Vortices. We know a few of these locations as:

- Mt. Shasta, California, USA
- The Great Pyramid at Giza, Egypt
- The Philippine Islands
- Vancouver Island, British Columbia, Canada
- Yucatan Peninsula, Mexico
- Philadelphia, Pennsylvania, USA
- The Azores of Portugal
- Lourdes, France
- Grand Teton, Wyoming, USA

As we begin to make our transitional shift in the expanding Law of Magnetic Love, new Golden Cities are activated to hold a finer consciousness for the new planet known as Freedom Star.

Following the Star

According to Hopi prophecies, the world existed three times before now. That is, it was created three different times in three different ways, by Taiowa, the Supreme Creator. Taiowa also destroyed these three former worlds when things didn't go the way he/she had planned. I won't go into great depth here, but I will lay some basic groundwork of the story so you'll gain a quick understanding. If you want to read the Hopi creation stories in their fullness (and I recommend you do) read *Book of the Hopi*, by Frank Waters.

The players in the Hopi creation story are Taiowa, Supreme Creator—generally referred to as a he—and the only creator in endless space. He creates a nephew, Sotuknang, who carries out his plans (his first lieutenant), and Sotuknang's helper, a her, Spider Woman. Her creative wisdom produces two twins, who help create the first world. After their work is done, the twins are sent to oversee each of the poles of the Earth; Poqanghoya to the north, and Palongawhoya to the south. Their creation story talks about light, sound, the axis of Earth and Earth's rotating position in the universe in relationship to the sun and the moon.

These prophecies are well over 10,000 years old! In 1492, we still thought the world was flat and the sea was filled with life-threatening sea monsters. The Hopi prophecies reflect scientific sophistication and abstract thinking.

The First World

The new world was very beautiful, with trees, flowers, animals, and birds, but Taiowa wanted a finishing touch. So Spider Woman created human beings, male and female. After their Chakra Systems were developed and they learned to speak, Creator gave them just one law to keep in order to live on and among his beautiful world. "Respect the Creator at all times," he said, "and have wisdom, harmony and respect for the love of the Creator who made you. May it grow and never be forgotten among you as long as you live." [6]

These first people were of many colors and understood their Mother Earth and Father Sun. They communicated with their Creator through their open doors, or the open seals of their chakras. They understood the Divine Power of each of their chakra centers, rarely knew sickness, and used crystals, if needed, for healing. Even though the first people spoke many different languages, they communicated with one another telepathically. They also communicated telepathically with birds and animals.

Unfortunately, it didn't last. The Oneness that they shared soon became divided with quarrels, suspicions, and judgments. The animals withdrew from the people and they couldn't communicate anymore. Everyone and everything became divided and the plan of the Creator was forgotten. Taiowa had no choice; he would have to destroy the world he had created. But there were still a few who had stayed open. They had followed the laws of the Creator and still communicated through their third eyes and Crown Chakras. They heard the voice of the Creator tell them to escape the upcoming destruction by following a Star to the inside of the Earth. This, they did, and when they were safe and sound inside, all of the volcanoes of the world erupted. An all-consuming fire engulfed and destroyed the first world and only the people inside the Earth were saved.

The Second World

When the people emerged into the second world, it was not quite as beautiful as the first. Although they no longer had the ability to communicate with the animals, they still had telepathic abilities with one another. Creator asked them to remember the old law, along with a new one . . . to sing with joy from their hearts about Creator.

The second world people multiplied, built homes and soon cities. They began to manufacture goods; they stored, saved, and established economies. Then, the trouble began.

More and more they manufactured things that weren't really needed. Soon, buying and selling and owning useless merchandise was more important than singing the joyful praises to Taiowa, the Creator. The second world became wicked and greedy; soon wars broke out. Again, the Creator had no choice but to destroy his creation. But, there was still a small group who sang the Creator's song, and again, they were led to the safety of the underground worlds. Taiowa gave his order to the twins. The poles shifted and the Earth was covered in ice. Mountains fell into oceans and seas. Lakes were frozen instantly. The Earth, silent and lifeless, waited for the birth of the third world.

The Third World

It took a long time for the third world to move; everything was frozen solid. After the twins got the poles adjusted and the Earth rotating properly, the ice melted and mountains and prairies emerged. Soon, it was time for the people inside the warm Earth to emerge. Again, they were given laws just like before. Taiowa asked them to keep the laws from the first and second worlds, to remember Creator and to sing joyful praises of Creator. But, they were also told to respect one another. These were their three laws.

Because the people had gained sufficient knowledge from the first two worlds, this time, they were highly evolved. They advanced quickly and soon populated the Earth again with numerous cities and countries. As more technology developed, the people of the third world realized it was harder to keep their chakras open and to communicate telepathically. Many people corrupted their Divine Energies and forgot to sing praises to Creator. Soon, they developed the ability to fly in the air (on patuwvotas, shields made of hide) and engaged in wars, city to city, country to country. The third world was very corrupt and this time it would be destroyed through water. Taiowa sent Spider Woman to talk to the people who still carried the Creator's song in their hearts. She taught them how to build large boats out of reeds. This, they did, and when their boats were sealed, the waters began to flood the world. The noise of the rushing waters was incredible. Large continents sunk and broke apart into small islands. Incredible rains fell. Then it stopped, and there was silence. The reed boats drifted the people over the silent waters for a long time. When their boats finally stopped on a new coastline, the people walked onto the dry lands for the first time. They had emerged into the fourth world. This is the world we are all living in today.

The Fourth World

The fourth world was very different than the other worlds. Creator told them that this world would not be as easy. It would have height and depth, heat and cold; in essence, it was a dual world. Through duality, we would learn how to make proper choices and only through our choices would we carry out the Creator's plan. The Hopi prophecies completely mirror the message of the I AM America Map and Freedom Star material. The references to choice, as being the pivotal spiritual law of the fourth world are prolific. There are virtually thousands of them, but here are a few strong examples, collected throughout the years:

"All that is, is through choice, and the responsibility of choice is yours." —*Sananda*

"For you see, Dear one, love may not enter your planet without choice. The hearts of men must allow love to stream forth. They must choose this love." —*Sananda*

"Come forward in a choice that is known of your own divinity. Come forward in a choice and see your perfection and you will have no doubt." —*Sananda*

"All of you have a choice and that choice is your experience. All of you may serve if you choose. Let this map awaken those to their Divine Choice!" —*Sananda*

"This divinity, God I AM, instills a deeper choice, for it resonates with a frequency you know as freedom . . . freedom is where you choose, freedom is that God I AM has given to each of you." —*Saint Germain*

"This is the Prophecy of destruction if not heeded. Understand, Dear children of my heart, that your choice and choosing make a difference." —*Kuan Yin*

"You do the choosing. We call each one of you, but you do the choosing. This is the gift of your free will." —*Saint Germain*

"Understand that this Earth Changes material, or shall we call it a Prophecy of choice, is brought to you so you may choose your eternal victory in this light." —*Saint Germain*

"It is only through choice that responsible freedom, then, is allowed to reign in this world of created forms. It is only through choice where men and women and children learn responsibility . . . this is the union of choices, for only in choice can responsibility begin. It is important to understand that these maps that have been presented are possibilities and potentials for creative change. While change is inevitable at this time and a change will come, the outcome lies in your hands. Lies in the responsibility of your choice." —*Saint Germain*

"As you are the human beings who have been given the God characteristics engendered in your will, since you carry the momentum of choice, you, Dear ones, are known as Co-creators." —*Saint Germain*

Migration and the Star of Self-Knowledge

There was another law that Creator's nephew, Sotuknang, gave the emerging peoples to live in the fourth world. "Now you will separate and go different ways to claim all the Earth for the Creator. Each group of you will follow your own Star until it stops. There you will settle." [7] Essentially, they were told to begin a migration. But, those migrations would begin by first following their own Stars, not a star in the sky, or an idea given them by someone else. The Star was theirs to discover and once discovered, theirs to lead them. The Star is located in each heart of the people of the fourth world. It is the Star of self-knowledge. It is found only through inner migration.

There are also many other references in the I AM America material to the process of inner migration and attainment of self-knowledge. These prophecies first appear to be literal. That is, moving, packing, and leaving an area. Read carefully, there is the hint of metaphor that the movement is also internal and is completely necessary.

"The time has come for you to move. Move not only from where you are living, but move into your heart. See that you serve that ONE great mighty force, I AM. Only in the service to the mighty force, I AM, will you find your eternal and infinite freedom. . . . Prophecy comes to this planet to open your eyes and open your ears. Primarily, it speaks to that Flame within your heart and you will know it is time for you to move." —*Saint Germain.*

Masaaw, the Spiritual Master

After Sotuknang gave the two new laws, choice and self-knowledge, he told the people that they would also be given guidance and help from spiritual deities. No sooner had Sotuknang disappeared, when a handsome man appeared. When the people asked who he was, he replied "My name is Masaaw." (Sounds alot like Master, doesn't it?)

Masaaw went on to explain, that, at one time, he had been appointed caretaker of the third world. He, too, along with the people, had misused his energies, but since he was an immortal being, he could not be destroyed. Instead, Creator assigned him to the underworld where he quickly got bored.

Taiowa decided to give him a second chance and appointed him a guardian and caretaker of the lands and people of the fourth world.

Now, many answers and questions about the Masters are probably in your mind. It is true, that the Masters continually give their guidance and helpfully ask, to "be of service." They also reside in retreats or areas that are under their focus or protective care. It is also apparent that they are immortal and they manifest in light bodies. They are also very beautiful and communicate telepathically, without using their voices. Maasaw, of the Hopi prophecies, very much resembles the Masters of the I AM America prophecies who are said to reside in fifty-one Golden Cities. Each of these spiritual beings is also a caretaker, much like Maasaw, over an area that is filled with their intentional focus and protection. The five Masters, or Maasaws, of the United States are El Morya, Kuthumi, Saint Germain, Sananda, and Serapis Bey. They protect their lands through spiritual ideals that they continuously transmit telepathically to the people of the fourth world. When you travel to the area they caretake, and your doors (or chakras) are open, you can receive their spiritual teaching if you choose. This is the gift of Taiowa and is the help that was promised from good spirits, in our journey in the fourth world.

The Five Stars of the United States

The Golden City of Gobean, is the first Spiritual Migration. The Teacher is El Morya and the lesson is inner peace, harmony, and personal transformation. Gobean is located in the Southwest.

The Golden City of Malton is the second Spiritual Migration. The teacher is Kuthumi and the lesson is attaining self-knowledge and communion with the elemental, devas, and nature spirits. Malton is located primarily in the state of Illinois and Indiana.

The Golden City of Wahanee is the third Spiritual Migration. The teacher is Saint Germain and the lesson is attaining full freedom through the understanding of personal justice and liberty of choice. Wahanee is located in the Southeast.

The Golden City of Shalahah is the fourth Spiritual Migration. The teacher is Sananda and the lesson is attaining the Creator's plan of abundance and prosperity through personal healing. Shalahah is located primarily in Montana and Idaho.

The Golden City of Klehma is the fifth Spiritual Migration. The teacher is Serapis Bey and the lesson is spiritual balance and harmony in groups. Klehma is located primarily in Colorado.

The I AM America Prophecies and the Seventeen Spiritual Migrations

There are forty-six other locations where Master Teachers work to help the people of the fourth world. You can read about them and their spiritual lessons in the book, *Freedom Star*. According to the I AM America prophecies, we have seventeen migrations (or spiritual teachings to understand) to complete our journey in the fourth world. If we choose this path, we then can help the Masters as Co-creators in the fifth world. But Maasaw gives a warning in the Hopi prophecies: "If you go back to your evil ways again, I will take over the earth from you, for I AM its caretaker, guardian and protector." [8] The seventeen migrations are for people all over the world and are identified in the *Freedom Star Earth Changes Map* and the *Freedom Star Book*.

The early people of the fourth world understood how important migration was and that it taught them how to rely on their Creator. They realized that since the test of this world was that it would be dual and always in contrast, that many of the places where they would be led to live would not be luxurious. Instead, the discomfort would allow their inner identity, or their Stars to emerge. The test this time was not to rely on materiality, but to gain all understanding through communication with the Creator. Through finding their Stars, Creator would always lead them to places that would always be for their best and highest good.

Masaaw tells the people in the Hopi prophecies, "You have not yet followed your Stars to the place where you will meet and settle. This you must do, before I can become your leader." [9] Today, we have forgotten our true inner identities as fourth world people. We live where it is most convenient, or where our jobs are, or where we like the weather. Very few of us have made the migrations that are necessary to complete the purpose of the fourth world. There are many lessons we can gain through intentional, Spiritual Migration . . . even if it is traveling to Augusta, Georgia, to receive insights on personal freedom or meditating every day on world peace. This work is very necessary if we are to create a new world, the fifth world.

The First Earth Changes Map

Before Masaaw left the people, he gave them specific outlines of where they were to migrate and how they were to live once they arrived at their destination. This was done symbolically on four stone tablets. These tablets are sacred to the Hopi, and several are still in existence today. There are pictures of these tablets in the book by Frank Waters, and there is one I think you'll find very fascinating. It is the tablet, the First Bear Clan tablet. (See diagram below.) When I saw it I immediately recognized it, as I work a lot with maps and cartography. Turn the figure upside down. There you will see an outline of Florida and the Georgia, North, and South Carolina coastlines. These areas are divided up for the migrations, much like counties divide our states today. To the east of northern Florida and Georgia, you'll note an island with lines radiating off of it. This is the continent of Atlantis, (in the same location as Atlantis on the I AM America Map), the place where the fourth world began its emergence and migrated from. This Prophecy accurately matches many teachings from the Masters that the red race's origin was Atlantis.

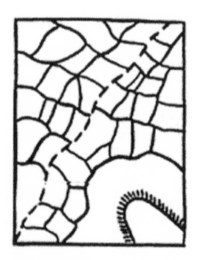

[DIAGRAM E: (Above) *A depiction from the Hopi Tablet.
From "The Book of the Hopi," by Frank Waters.*]

Time Frames

I've done a little research on eastern Indian time-keeping systems, (If you want to read more on this subject, see the book *Freedom Star*, pages 72–3.) It is a system based on yugas (time frames) with each yuga carrying distinct characteristics. (The time frames for the Yuga System is classic Hindu—not Sri Yuteswar's Electric Cycle which places the beginning of Dvapara Yuga and the end of Kali Yuga in 1700 AD)

2.2 million years BC—Treta Yuga begins. This is the rise and fall of Lemuria. This is the first world.

867,102 BC—Dvapara Yuga begins. The civilization of Mu (located in the now South Pacific) begins; the emergence of the second world. The continent of Atlantis rises.

15,000 BC—Ice Age, Mu Sinks. This is the end of the second world.

9,628 BC—Atlantis sinks. (Although Atlantis is said to have sunk in three parts, I estimate this is the timing of its final demise.) This is the end of the third world and the birth of the fourth world.

3,102 BC—Kali Yuga begins. Spider woman loses her immortality, and the world becomes dominated by masculine energy.

360 BC—Plato writes about the lost continent of Atlantis.

[Editor's Note: To learn more about timelines and the metaphysical history of Ancient Earth, see *Divine Destiny: Prophecies and Teachings for the New Times from the Ascended Masters.*]

The Blue Star

There are many more interesting correlations between the ancient Hopi prophecies and the I AM America material. One of the most intriguing prophecies is the appearance of the Blue Star. The Hopi prophecies state that when the Blue Star appears, that spiritual beings will destroy the conflict between material and spiritual concerns and create a new world aimed toward the laws and unity of the Creator. "The time is not far off. It will come when the Saquasohuh, (Blue Star), Kachina dances in the plaza. He represents a Blue Star, far off and yet invisible, which will make its appearance soon."[10] Again, note the reference to the word "star" and also to the Blue Star Kachina.

In the I AM America and Freedom Star Earth Changes prophecies, there are fifty-one Golden City Vortices. Although they span of over 250 miles across, the Vortices are invisible to the naked eye, but to a person whose chakras are open, or is sensitive to Earth energy, they are very detectable. Often, the Master Teachers refer to the apexes of the Vortices as the Stars. The Star of every Golden City Vortex is forty miles in diameter, with the apex in the center. Some of the locations of the apexes are pinpointed with great accuracy. Some are not.

The Stars of the Golden City Vortices play an important role in the Time of Change as these are areas where the Masters, or Masaaws, are prophesied to appear. It is prophesied after their appearance, they will reside in visible, physical bodies, teaching and healing those who come.

El Morya, the Blue Star Kachina

Each Master, or Masaaw, represents the focus of a Ray Force. Some folks say that the Rays represent the seven planets. Alice Bailey has compiled some of the best material I've read concerning the esoteric influences of Ray Forces. But, in terms of understanding a more exoteric approach to Rays and their meanings, I suggest you read any book by A.D.K. Luk or pick up *The Gnosis and the Law*, by Tellis S. Papastavro. According to Ascended Master traditions, the Blue Ray holds the qualities of illumined faith, and will . . . choice. Is that starting to sound familiar? There is only one Master strong enough to hold the characteristics of such a Ray: Master El Morya, Chohan of the Blue Ray, and protector of the first Golden City, Gobean.

El Morya was the Rajput prince and teacher to H.P. Blavatsky. He often appears in dreams and visions to those he has chosen to teach. When he was known as Mahatma Morya to Madame Blavatsky in the 1850s he was well over 125 years old and looked not a day over 30! He often used the name Ahazhulama, the Hindu name for Blue Teacher. El Morya is the prophet, the spiritual being, the Master, the Blue Star Kachina prophesied by the Hopis!

It is interesting to note, that many of the lands that Master El Morya oversees as caretaker and protector in the Golden City Vortex of Gobean are lands that were originally held by the Hopi. Gobean is prophesied to be the first Golden City Vortex to be activated and the first to manifest its teacher.

Questions and Answers

Q: Is the I AM America Map the Hopi Map mentioned in the teachings of Kryon?

A: While there are startling correlations between the Hopi prophecies and the I AM America Map, they are not related. The I AM America Map is sponsored by the Great White Lodge or Great White Brotherhood.

It is interesting to note, that the Hopis are a culture of people who have already made their migrations, literally and metaphorically. The I AM America material is an awakening call from the Masters to those who have yet to make their Spiritual Migrations.

Q: The Hopi prophecies speak about Pahana, the lost white brother. Is this related?

A: It may be so. It is interesting to note that the I AM America material is sponsored by the Great White Brotherhood. It is a Prophecy that, if completed with responsible choice, is aimed toward the same goals as the ancient people of the fourth world: peace and universal Brotherhood. It is a plan of Brotherhood that may be birthed out of cataclysm, or may be birthed out of love. That choice and outcome is inevitably up to all of us.

> "The song resounds back from our Creator with joy,
> and we of the Earth repeat it to our Creator.
> At the appearing of the yellow light,
> Repeats and repeats again the joyful echo,
> Sounds and resounds for times to come."
> -from *The Song of Creation* [11]

The Eight-Sided Cell of Perfection and the Movement through the Nine Perfections

Feng Shui is an ancient practice that analyses the celestial heavens and their unique timing alongside dynamic landform to create harmonizing architecture and interiors. Taoist tradition describes this as the pattern of wind and water, and the beginning of this form of ancient Shamanism dates around 2200 BC. Its Hindu cousin Vastu is based on sacred texts known as Shastras that describe the four elements of: earth (Bhumi); water (Jal); light or fire (Agni); air (Vayu); and undifferentiated space (Akasha).

Understanding and Mastering the movement of these forces was an important aspect of the role of ancient leaders and early Chinese Shaman-Kings. Eva Wong writes of this remarkable history in her book, *Feng Shui, The Ancient Wisdom of Harmonious Living for Modern Times,* "The ancient shaman-kings' Mastery of the elements can also be attributed to their knowledge of land forms and weather. Fog, cloud, mist, and rain are associated with certain geographical features, and the king was expected to lead his tribe safely through treacherous terrain." [12]

These remarkable systems track energy movement on Mother Earth and when we honor and balance these forces in our homes and businesses, the science of the five elements (known as earth, water, fire, air, and metal in the Chinese system) produce nourishment, blessings, and balance in our lives. In this Time of Great Change, comprehension of the primal forces of life and nature initiates our consciousness to a spacious spectrum of the unseen order, and prepares one for Unana, Unity Consciousness, and the birth of the Fourth and Fifth Dimensions.

"We live in an amazing matrix of forces," writes William Levacy in *Beneath a Vedic Sky*, "Many of which the Vedic literature hints at, but Western science has yet to discover or understand. It's easy to see that if we are in proper alignment with these forces, much like being oriented correctly with a river's current, we will benefit. If we are misaligned and out of phase with the solar and geomagnetic forces, we can imagine and experience how dysfunctional and arrhythmic our life has become." [13] The principle of sattva in Hindu means pure and unadulterated. The Buddhist principle of sattva, once explained by Kuan Yin, means harmonious response to vibration or rhythm. There is a perfected outcome in understanding and applying this profound knowledge.

One basis of Feng Shui or Vastu relies
language contained within the pa-kua (also call
directions. The Master Teachers refer to this as t
Perfection and the nine-directions as the Nine F
the pa-kua contains nine palaces. In Vastu, energ
directions and the center is Brahma, Lord of Cre
the Master Teachers, the Eight-sided cell of Perfe
at a cellular and metaphoric, spiritual level. This
awakening process and directs our consciousness and spiritual growth
and development. Interestingly, the Eight-sided Cell mirrors the micro-
cosm of the structure of the Golden City Vortex. This shape and its inherent energetic movement play a significant role in both our individual
and global spiritual growth and development into the New Times.

Here are descriptions of the Nine Perfections. Since our homes
mirror our state of consciousness, you can overlay this system over the
floor-plan of your home to gain spiritual insight. This same system also
works as a greater macrocosm and overlays every Golden City Vortex.
Displaying the shamanic energy flow of each Ascended Master's Golden
City Vortex, this system also maps vital lei lines and meridians. And
if you want to learn more about the Eight-sided Cell of Perfection, I
suggest that you read the first three books of the Golden City Series:
Points of Perception, *Light of Awakening*, and *Divine Destiny*. There you
will find many teachings with correlating illustrations and diagrams.
For now, here are some introductory basics on the Nine Perfections and
their sacred directions, along with their color Rays and inherent qualities.

First Perfection: Temple of Being. Direction: Center. Colors:
Green, White. Spiritual fire, heart, and health.

Second Perfection: Divine Purpose. Direction: South. Colors:
Brown, Red, Gold. Self-expression.

Third Perfection: Marriage. Direction: Southeast. Colors: Olive, Pink, Platinum. Sharing and mate.

Fourth Perfection: Family. Direction: Southwest. Colors: Sage,
Ruby, Diamond. The World in Cosmic Motion.

...ction: Children. Direction: East. Colors: Aqua, Blue,
Generation through nature.

...ixth Perfection: Spirit Guides. Direction: Northeast. Colors:
Aqua Green, Light Blue, Purple. Spiritual teachers.

Seventh Perfection: Abundance. Direction: North. Colors:
Green, Sky Blue, Black. Money and Growth.

Eighth Perfection: Career. Direction: Northwest. Colors: Grey,
Turquoise, Navy Blue. The World (Illusion).

Ninth Perfection: Star of Knowledge. Direction: West. Colors:
Spring Green, Sunshine Yellow, and Gold-White. Choice.

Alongside the system of the Nine Perfections, the Master
Teachers map subtle energy changes within each doorway of a Golden
City Vortex. I will share these four gateways later.

Cities of Gold

The myth of cities made of gold is an old one. In fact, the story may have started as a rumor by a group of eighth-century Spanish bishops. While fleeing the invading Moors, they sailed westward, across the Atlantic Ocean where they claimed they encountered a paradise, Seven Cities of Gold.

The experience left a lasting impression and after their return to Spain, they insisted that, "Even the sands were made of gold."[14]

Perhaps it was this vision of paradise but, more likely it was greed that inspired the sixteenth-century explorations of North America's Southwest by Spanish explorers Cortez and Coronado. Their insatiable thirst for the worldly riches contained in the fabled Seven Cities of Cibola most likely contributed to the savage slaughter of thousands of indigenous peoples. The Seven Cities have never been found but speculation places them in two likely places: the Four Corners area of Arizona and New Mexico and the now present-day location of the City of Phoenix, The Valley of the Sun.

History documents the richness of the Ancient Valley of the Sun, but the remnants of a once sophisticated canal system and ball courts of the Hohokham are indeed small when compared to what might have existed. Travel north, above present-day Fountain Hills near Phoenix on the Beeline Highway, and you will notice acres of large boulders, smoothly pronouncing themselves among an occasional saguaro or ocotillo cactus. Quite honestly, it looks like a forgotten warzone. According to historian Richard Petersen, that may be exactly what it is, but it was not destruction by nuclear weapons. Rather, a comet's wrath may have struck around 1680 AD. In Petersen's opinion, what was destroyed was a fabulous, gold-laden Hohokham city filled with mines, workers, and fine artists of the precious metal.[15] Golden Cities are also spoken about in the Book of Revelation, and it was one of seven angels, in Saint John's well documented vision, who gave him a tour. John described the great city as "The holy Jerusalem, descending out of heaven from God."[16] The Angel guiding John was thorough. Together they measured and documented the size of the city and counted three seamless pearl gateways on each of the four directions. Precious stones of sapphire and emerald encrust the walls of the foundation of the city. Even its streets are constructed of gold, "And the street of the city was pure gold, as (if) it were transparent glass."[17] John noticed several quali-

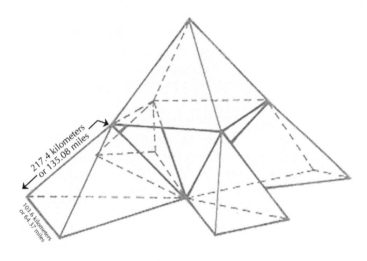

217.4 kilometers or 135.08 miles

103.6 kilometers or 64.37 miles

[DIAGRAM F: (Above) *Structure of the Golden City Vortex.*]

ties in his visit of this great city. Without clergy or temples, it seemed to continuously radiate God's loving energy and was uninterruptedly filled with light, "I saw no temple therein: for the Lord God Almighty and the Lamb are the temple of it. And the city had no need of the sun, neither of the moon, to shine in it; for the glory of God did lighten it, and the Lamb is the light thereof." And he continues in more wonderful description, "And the gates of it shall not be shut at all by day: for there shall be no night there,"[18] suggesting that this continuously open city is to be utilized by all who come and not just a select few. Its creation is perfect and the intention of its usage appears universal. The Golden Cities of the Ascended Masters' I AM America prophecies are not encrusted with jewels or filled with streets paved with gold, but much like the city of John's vision in the Book of Revelation, their gates are always open and their presence meant for all. They constantly radiate a high spiritual energy and in the New Times are prophesied to play a large role in the creation of universal Brotherhood and Sisterhood.

The Masters were very specific in describing the structure of a Golden City Vortex. (See diagram F.): 3-sided tetrahedrons create a foundation for a pyramidal apex.) They described its sacred shape as built upon a series of pyramids. Its symbology reinforces how man's consciousness, at this time, is evolving from a Third-Dimensional orientation to Fourth and Fifth Dimensional awareness. Saint Germain's introductory information about Golden Cities refers to these areas as protected and says that they would serve as a focus for "interaction with spiritual energy."[19]

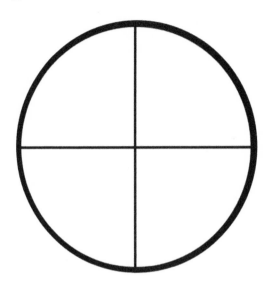

[DIAGRAM G: (Above) *Ancient symbol for a Vortex.*]

Researchers of Vortices would most likely agree. Richard Dannelley, Sedona Vortex authority, says that a Vortex of Earth's energy, "Allows power from the dimension of pure energy to leak through into our dimension."[20] Vortices seem to appear at intersections of the Earth's grid, or biomagnetic field of the Earth. These intersecting strands of Earth's energy are also known as lei lines. The symbol for a Vortex is a cross in a circle. (See diagram G.) Dannelley writes of this symbol, "The cross is the symbol of the union of cosmic forces, the coming together of the polarities which create the world. A cross may be defined as a Vortex: The intersection of angles. In the practice of geomancy a cross is used to mark a place where the strands of the Web of Life join together, thus forming a Power Spot."[21] The Ascended Masters have marked each prophesied Golden City Vortex with a similar symbol. (See diagram H.)

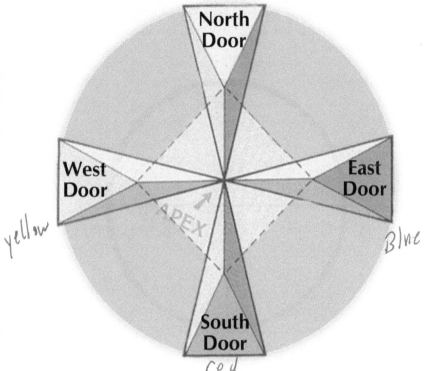

Black

yellow

Blue

red

[DIAGRAM H: (Above) *Ascended Master symbol for a Golden City Vortex. This illustration also depicts the four doors of a Golden City Vortex.*]

According to the Master Teachers, a Golden City Vortex works on the principle of electromagnetism, but the surrounding geology is also key to understanding this natural phenomenon. Research is proving that Vortices seem to appear near fault lines and that they may be channeling energies of the inner Earth. (i.e., Gobean Vortex: Mogollon Rim; Malton Vortex: New Madrid Fault line; Shalahah Vortex: a rediscovered ancient fault line near the Snake River and Hells Canyon causes a surprise earthquake in 1998.[22]) Basalt pillars and ancient lava deposits with their high iron content are also natural conductors of electromagnetic energies. It is a proven scientific fact that igneous rocks are much more strongly magnetized than sedimentary rocks. The presence of basalt and rocks with high iron content is visibly apparent at Mount Baldy, Arizona (the apex of the Gobean Golden City Vortex)

and throughout the Gobean Vortex. This is also true of th
Vortex of Shalahah (in Idaho and Montana). Water is als
and may play a role in the disbursement of Vortex energ
the Gobean Vortex is the largest aquifer in the Southwe
freshwater lakes, Coeur d'Alene and Pend 'Orielle in Idaho and …
head Lake in Montana, are located in the Shalahah Vortex. I'm sure if
all of the Golden City Vortices were researched in this manner, this list
would prove endless.

Vortices that spin clockwise take energy in; counterclockwise,
energy is released. Their movement is mirrored in nature: funnel-like,
devastating, and powerful tornadoes; twisting beautiful seashells; and
simple dishwater going down the drain. Scientifically, a Vortex is a
polarized motion body which creates its own magnetic field, aligning
molecular structures with phenomenal accuracy. "Nature has basically
two types of motion. One is centripetal and the other centrifugal. These
motions have a definite geometrical pattern when they are generated by
natural means. This geometrical form is call 'The Vortex.' A Vortex is
the three-dimensional form by which all mediums like water, air, solids,
electricity and magnetism, sound, light, etc. are generally maintained
and dissipated. They give birth to and disperse our planet and all particles of matter."[23]

When the Golden City Vortex shape is laid out in a plain view,
a new perspective emerges. What is now seen is four directions—gateways or doorways as defined by the Master Teachers. On a simplistic
level, the doors are the directions from which we enter the Golden City,
but the doorway that we enter from may have a powerful, spiritual
meaning.

At an esoteric level, the four directions symbolize four spiritual
pathways we can choose. Commenting on "The Most Holy Trinosophia," one of the few manuscripts known to be written by Saint Germain more than 100 years ago to prepare his chelas in the cabalistic,
hermetic, and alchemical mysteries, Manly Hall writes, "The doors
signify the courses which the soul can pursue. The black door is the
path of asceticism and labor; the red door is that of faith; the blue door
is that of purification, and the white door is that of adeptship and of the
highest Mysteries. In the Bhagavad-Gita, Krishna describes these paths
and those who follow them, and reveals that the last is the highest and
most perfect."[24] The Golden Cities of the I AM America prophecies

ent the power of choice and its ability to overcome the adversity
catastrophe presented in the Earth Changes prophecies. Master K.
H. clearly states, "Within your heart lies the gentle revolution which
can redirect the course of such events."[25] The four doors are an integral
part of the spiritual and alchemical teachings of I AM America and the
Golden Cities. Here are their descriptions:

The Northern Door, also known as the black door, represents discipline and hard labor. Kuan Yin lends spiritual insight to this
concept: "If you are to travel to the northern portion of the Vortex, you
will find that you will be asked to transmute and forgive."[26] However,
as these Golden City energies are absorbed and integrated, worldly
benefits can emerge. Northern Doors are said to bring our desires
into fruition and manifest physical abundance. In the New Times it is
prophesied that the energies of the Northern Doors will produce the
most abundant and prolific food crops and are the best locations for
commercial and business endeavors.

The Southern Door, also known as the red door, represents
the Healing of the Nations through enlightened love, non-judgment,
faith, and courage. Energies of this door are good for healing at any
level—body, mind, and spirit. In the New Times it is prophesied that
many miracle healings will be demonstrated in these areas, and because
of the natural, beneficial energies, they are good locations for hospitals,
healing clinics, retreats, and spas. The energies of Southern Doors are
also said to assist in physical regeneration.

The Eastern Door is also known as the blue door. Its energies
demand purification and sacrifice but, with the great reward of Alchemy. Saint Germain refers to the path of the Eastern Door as "The Elixir
of Life." The blue door also signifies friends, family, and those who are
helpful. The Master Teachers claim that any relationship or family prob-
lem can be solved through time spent in contemplation on or in this
doorway. In the New Times, it is prophesied that the Eastern Doors of
the Golden City Vortices are perfect locations for communities, group
activities, residential homes, and schools for young children.

The Western Door. In the I AM America teachings, the
Western Door is known as the yellow door. It is the path of wisdom,
and is sometimes called "The Philosopher's Stone." It is also said to be
the path of adeptship and perfection and is often the conclusion of
the four pathways before entry into the "Star of Knowledge." Western

Doors are good locations for universities and schools of higher and spiritual knowledge. The Master Teachers claim that in the New Times, all governmental activities should be located within the energies of the Western Doors.

The Star

The center of each Golden City Vortex is called The Star. The path of The Star is ideally the "Star of Self-Knowledge." Living in a Star area will produce self-knowledge and self-empowerment. The Star is by far, one of the most powerful areas of a Golden City Vortex and since all four energies of the doorways coalesce throughout, it is identified with the color white. Stars of Golden City Vortices are said to be forty miles in diameter—but the benefits of this radius can be felt for up to sixty miles. In the New Times, the Stars will be used as ceremonial grounds and their energies are good for self-renunciation, meditation, and spiritual liberation. It is also prophesied that during the Times of Changes, the energies of the Stars will become so purified and beneficially charged that this is where the Master Teachers will be able to manifest in physical form. It is then prophesied that much spiritual teaching and more miracle healing will occur.

Communities of the New Times

In the Earth Changes prophecies, the Ascended Masters have shared that five population areas of the United States will emerge in the New Times (see "Prophecies of Political and Social Change from the I AM America Material"), centering around the five Golden Cities. In the *New York Times* bestseller, *The Roaring 2000s*, author and economic forecaster Harry Dent correlates this interesting Prophecy in his chapter on the next great population shift and real estate boom: He predicts that twelve states are at the top of the list to add population between the years of 1995 to 2015. Interestingly, Arizona (Gobean) is number four; Georgia (Wahanee) is number five; North Carolina (Wahanee) is number seven; and Colorado (Klehma) is number eight!

Dent's provocative book also outlines the upcoming "Right Brain Revolution" and correlates this shift in human development to four stages developed by the founding father of modern psychology, Abraham Maslow. Maslow's famous Hierarchy of Human Needs illustrates that as we move from a survival stage, which focuses on basic needs such as food and water, we become less need directed. We move to a second stage of consciousness, which is defined as belonging, socializing, and building relationships with others. This outer-directed urge develops into the third stage of self-esteem. At this level or stage of consciousness, the individual is focused upon self-respect, achievement, status, recognition, attention, and leadership. At the fourth and final, or highest, stage that Maslow observed is the inner-directed consciousness of self-actualization. Dent predicts that right now we are witnessing the "Most massive advance in human psychology and development in history, but not without chaos and confusion," as one of the largest population groups, the Baby Boomers, makes massive shifts into the higher Maslow stages.

Throughout all of the I AM America prophecies and spiritual teachings, the Ascended Masters have spoken about the remarkable changes in human psychology and needs that will occur as we progress into the New Times. Often, they simply call this, "The New Consciousness." The energies of the Golden City Vortices also play a role in assisting this awakening. Since each Golden City has certain and subtle energies working through specific Ray Forces and Ascended Masters, this assistance reinforces spiritual growth and self-development to the higher, fourth-level Maslow stage of self-actualization. It is then prophesied that humanity will make a tremendous growth collectively and enter into a new dimension of consciousness and expression beyond the four Maslow stages. This is what is known as the Ascension Process.

Beyond the higher Maslow stages of human development, the Ascended Masters have shared that existence is defined through Unity Consciousness or what they call the state of Unana. In this higher state of consciousness, human cells (DNA) become perfected and the light energy within the body reaches a point where the light bodies (aura) exceed the physical body. David Hudson's provocative research on superconductivity and the Miessner Field states, "You literally light up the room when you walk in. You are a light being, your mind is ONE with other people's minds. You literally know their thoughts and they know your thoughts. You're ONE mind and you are ONE heart."[27]

In the I AM America information, the energies of the Golden City Vortices, when properly understood and applied, are prophesied to propel consciousness through the Fourth and Fifth Dimensions where we can experience perfect telepathy; full use of the brain (we only use fifteen percent); physical regeneration; spontaneous healing; instant thought manifestation; and bi-location. Beloved Sananda often reminds us, "The minutes and the seconds tick, the Awakening is at hand. The time has come for man to receive the gift!"

Golden Cities function like large, intentional communities of electromagnetic energy. They are very expansive, when compared to the size of a town or city, spanning almost 400 kilometers in diameter and over 200 miles high. Their influence is not intended for a select or small group. When understood in this context, it is clear that the energies of Golden Cities are meant to influence many peoples, regardless of race, nationality, gender, or religious affiliation. But what exactly is an intentional community? Geoph Kozeny, community expert, coordinator and writer for *Communities Magazine*, defines an intentional community as, "A group of people who have chosen to live together with a common purpose, working cooperatively to create a lifestyle that reflects their shared core values. The people may live together on a piece of rural land, in a suburban home, or in an urban neighborhood, and they may share a single residence or live in a cluster of dwellings."[28]

The history of intentional communities is extensive and not limited to sixties dropout communes. They range from the Essenes, to fourteenth-century Hutterians, Amish, Quakers, artists, back to the land survivalists. Even the early followers of Jesus banded together to simplify their lives. One very interesting intentional community of our times is the Findhorn Community located in northeast Scotland.

While the original founders, Peter and Eileen Cady and Dorothy Maclean, did not intend to start a community in Findhorn, Morayshire, they were brought together in 1962 as part of their individual commitment to follow God's will. Once settled, their early work included direct communication and cooperation with the kingdoms of nature (devas and elementals) that led to the development of their world-renowned gardens. David Spangler joined the group in 1970 and soon the educational aspects were organized into a curriculum that established a University of Light, welcoming guests to learn about and experience the God within. Today, approximately 450 people reside in Findhorn and the Findhorn Foundation supports worldwide efforts in the areas of organic and sustainable agriculture, reforestation, ecological architecture, alternative energy, resource conservation, and holistic health care.

In the 1940s, Paramahansa Yogananda of the Self-Realization Fellowship proposed the formation of "World Brotherhood Communities" to practice "simple living and high thinking." In 1968, his disciple Kiryananda created Ananda Village on 700 acres of land. Yogananda always stressed that "Environment is stronger than will power," suggesting that like-minded souls on a similar spiritual path could create the ideal atmosphere for healing, personal change, and self-improvement. Yogananda wrote in *Autobiography of a Yogi*, "A small harmonious group here may inspire other ideal communities over the earth. A colony exemplifying world Brotherhood is empowered to send inspiring vibrations far beyond its locale."[29]

Most intentional communities seem by inspiration to reflect certain religious or spiritual teachings. The Golden City Vortices also encourage and foster spiritual growth and personal development and offer a unique anomaly. The architecture of the massive, pyramidal Vortices is designed by the Ascended Masters in cooperation and harmony with Mother Earth. Saint Germain reflects on this profound truth in this 1989 Earth Changes Prophecy, "The surface of this planet has offered herself to assist in the cleansing of the lower bodies of mankind." The sacred symbology of the Golden Cities reinforces how man's consciousness, at this time, is evolving from a Third Dimensional orientation to Fourth and Fifth Dimensional awareness. Introductory information about Golden Cities always refers to these areas as "protected" and says that they will serve as a focus for "interaction with spiritual energy."

CHAPTER FIVE

Spiritual Teachings

Desire that Co-Creates the Love of God by Master K. H.
Many students on the path have argued about desire. Some find it to be the source of all discomfort—their commitment to holding their passions in bondage. Others find desire to be like detecting the scent of the flowers; they use desire as the indicator, much like a thermometer on a frozen winter morning, to show the true feelings if the heart. My teacher once spoke of it this way: "Desire! The giver and glory of pain and love. Once I Master you, I face the truth of the Universe!" Desire is the giver and glory of pain and love, and it is the measure of our spiritual agility. Desire can lead us temporarily off of the path or startlingly push us back on.

Desire inevitably, returns us to the creative force, the Omnipresent source. When we become frozen or weak in our journey here, we can rest assured desire will return us to our home. All, who are created from the love that fills all of life, yearn to return to that love. From the point of love within the heart of God, we travel throughout the worlds of form, seeking protection and union through the love that created us. It is with the desire for the love of God that I shall begin this lesson. Open your hearts, and perhaps you will feel the fluttering of the pure Flame of Desire.

A young student traveled the path until he met a man he knew would be his guru. He followed the teacher like a lost puppy, begging him to take him into his study. Soon, the teacher, wearied by the young man's constant attention, asked him to follow him to the river. Both walked out to waist-deep water, and the teacher quickly plunged the head of the young man under until he kicked and bubbled for life-giving air! When the teacher finally let him up, the young student, gasping for breath and after several minutes of shock and disbelief, asked the older man, "Why did you do that?" Then the wise man replied, "When you desire God, like you desired that breath of air while you were under the water, you are ready then to follow the path with me."

Desire works this way for all of us. Leading us innocently into waters, fires, and earthquakes; and desire which greed, ambition, or avarice - upon reflection and experience once fueled - seeks purification. Initiation, through desire, is the most tempered of fires but also the most essential. There will be many fires that you will walk through while you travel the path. The path is strewn with broken dreams and unfulfilled expectations, all discarded when realized they are the frivolous garments covering the prize inside, the fruit of the nut, the Omnipotent truth.[30] It is truth that we come to value as stalwart followers of the path and plan.

We are created of this truth and while we desire to hold it unto ourselves, we cannot. For that would destroy us.

Yet truth universally brings us all to the understanding of the causeless cause and evolves to hold the spark of desireless desire.

When we can serve that cause without expectations or personal desire, we serve from the point that we departed from. This is the point of love and truth and we accept our role as a Co-creator, mirrored in the image and likeness of our creator.

The Five-Fold Path

Those of you who accept the role of servant, expect but one thing, you will know freedom. Your purpose is to serve the will of God through humanity and the worlds of form. Your desireless form will know the Christ and you will build the bridge between the worlds of form and spirit. Through your open eyes you will open the doors of the soul. Through your open ears you will attain perception. Carry always the symbol of the Star, for you are Divine Man!

Should you walk the path of the teacher, profess your service to all of life! Through synchronicity, thought, and meditation you become the awakener. You will know the ONE, the consciousness of ALL and there will be your source of inspiration and experience. Allow the upper lid of your all-seeing eye to be the teacher, allow the lower lid to be the student. Be watchful that you do not become too narrow or slanted, but keep your eyes wisely open. Upon your shoulder rests the owl, you who hold the eyes for humanity to recognize divinity for all.

Should you walk the path of the healer, you will hold the keys to understand desire through the development of the senses, compassion, and the intelligence of diagnosis. You will profess to the wholeness of body and mind as a Peaceful Warrior who carries a sword of love that applies and directs energy. Your source is the Mother God who knows only purification and sacrifice joined with the great reward of Alchemy. You walk the path in service to divinity, knowing that the light that shines, shines for all as ONE. As the healed carry the potency of the healer, you carry the potency of those healed. The swirling circles of LIFE continuous - the lotus and the rose - are your symbols.

Should you walk the path of the prophet, know that your purpose is for the healing of the nations. You will constantly be a catalyst who will work with the tools of consciousness for change and choice. Check carefully at all times your intent; dilute it not, for your skill lies in the strength of your balance and interpretation. You know your source as spirit and seek the equalization in divinity—as above, so below. Once you choose this path, do not turn back. "Great ones fall back even from the threshold unable to sustain the weight of their responsibility, unable to pass on. Therefore, look forward always with awe and trembling to this moment and be prepared for the battle."[31] The path of the prophet purposely surrenders all lower desires; its symbol is the dove of peace.

Should you walk the path of the priest, know that your purpose will seal divinity. Through ceremony, prayer, and song you transform and harmonize, knowing your source as the Father God. You are the leader of the groups who also knows and understands the sound of silence. "Listen only to the voice which is soundless. Look only on that which is invisible alike to the inner and the outer sense."[32] You flow within; and you flow without. You tread the path of the adept, seeking and knowing only perfection. You are the perfect man, known through ancient numerology in the number 9. You are the animal 666, (6+6+6=18=9) who has chosen to regenerate, 144,000 (1+4+4+0+0+0=9). Your symbol is the Tree of Life and the Philosopher's Stone.

Let me tabulate again this five-fold path of desire, should you choose to tread:

Servant................. "The working of the Divine Plan."
Teacher................ "The recognition of Divinity."
Healer.................. "The service to Divinity."
Prophet................ "The equalization in Divinity."
Priest................... "The sealing of Divinity."

The Course of Service Is Required

Know that each of these courses is required in the journey on the path. Each of them is streamed and fueled by desire, and inevitably leads us back to the source of CREATOR LOVE. So that we know the truth of desireless desire, we approach each of these roles through embodiment after embodiment, through the service of the Rays and the roles of desire that we choose. In our mission to know truth, each role, much like the Rays, presents itself in service to the next. For instance, the role of the servant paves the pathway for the teacher; the teacher paves the pathway for the healer; the healer paves the pathway for the prophet; the prophet paves the pathway for the priest; and the priest paves the pathway for the adept, he who listens to the voice of silence.

In many instances, we blend the roles of desire, seeking an understanding of TRUTH and LIFE, much as the Rays blend their septenary qualities for our sacred mission. To gain a better understanding of the correlation between the Rays and the roles of desire, I present this table:

Servant................... Rays Blue and White
Teacher................... Rays Pink and Yellow
Healer..................... Rays Pink, Yellow, and Green
Prophet................... Rays Yellow, White, and Red
Priest...................... Rays Green, Red, and Violet

The student on the path chooses one or several of these forms of selfless service to understand the role of desire and the evolution of the mighty spark of OMNISCIENCE. Gently and gracefully, when the student intentionally chooses to drop self-centeredness to the call of service on the path, he holds the keys to emergent evolution. When the HU-man, Divine God, being can no longer be denied expression, the hold that the animal consciousness once held, drops into slumber. This

wow — like a relay!

great victory achieved allows a greater service. The call of the Lodge, dedicated to the service and spiritual upliftment of humanity, opens your ears.

An Invitation

I close by extending an invitation to all of you to join with us. The need is great among humanity today. There is still needless suffering fueled by the fires of ignorance and deception. Quietly listen and you will hear the call in your heart. We are not a religious group or sect. However, we are a service group of elder Brothers and Sisters who have been known through mankind's history as the Great White Lodge. Through the medium of consciousness we have merged our efforts and energies aimed toward the unity of all of life. Our goal is simple, and our work is hard. It is never promised to be easy; however, the reward is immeasurable. Come, through prayer and meditation, if you feel the urge of the mission within.

A new cycle awaits humanity. It is a cycle filled with growth, learning, and life. Painfully and lovingly, sometimes this growth is achieved through disease, poverty, and destruction. However, within your heart lies the gentle revolution, which can redirect the course of such events.

This is a revolution armed with the power of service, charity, and love. If you should turn your back, know that timelessly we await.

Let us join in wisdom to extinguish ignorance and inequity.

Let us join in love to extinguish suffering.

Let us join in service to extinguish greed and avarice.

Let us join in charity to extinguish poverty.

Let us join in harmony to extinguish disease.

As our ears are opened and our eyes begin to see, let is join as ONE LIGHT, in our hearts and minds. May this light of wisdom serve all. May this light of truth and justice prevail. May the law be written in hearts and joined through harmony, Brotherhood, and love.

Timelessly and agelessly, the unknown poet sings, "O, let not the flame die out! Cherished age after age in its dark cavern—in its holy temples cherished. Fed by pure ministers of love—let not the flame die out!"

OM MANAYA PITAYA HITAKA!

(I AM the Light of God, So Be It)

~Master K.H., a member and servant of the Great White Lodge

Seven Rays of Light and Sound

Light and sound are the core of classic Ascended Master education and are often presented through teachings on the Rays. Understanding the Rays and utilizing them opens our world to new potential and possibility and guides our entry into the fascinating world of Co-Creation—a restorative and sacred journey, including access to super senses, telepathy, clairvoyance, clairaudience, spontaneous healing, and Unity Consciousness.

What Is a Ray?

Simply stated, a Ray is a force containing a purpose that divides its efforts into two measurable and perceptible powers: light and sound. Alice Bailey writes in *Esoteric Psychology*, "A Ray is but a name for a particular force or type of energy, with the emphasis upon the quality which that force exhibits and not upon the form aspect which it creates. This is a true definition of a ray."[33]

Light and sound are the building blocks of our universe and everything in our world of thought, feeling, and action contains them. The Human Aura contains the twin matrix powers of light and sound, and often a healer with developed psychic abilities will note certain colors and sound frequencies in the aura of a patient when rendering a diagnosis. Nature mimics a similar variety. Plants bloom in an array of colorful flowers; minerals grow into brilliant crystal facets of emerald, ruby, or diamond; and the sweet serenade of each bird is a melody that is distinct and characteristic to its particular species. Each specific color and sound in our universe carries a certain vibration, creating and producing different results.

In various world cultures, light and sound invoke different attributes and properties that have meaning and import to that society. Throughout the European-influenced Western culture, black is often associated with dark and evil and is a color of mourning and worn at funerals. Yet, in many Native American traditions, black represents the Great Mystery and is the color often associated with north. In Eastern cultures, white is often worn at funerals, however in the West, it is often worn at wedding ceremonies. Sound, too, has difference meanings in different cultures. Imagine European settlers hearing what they thought were the unsettling pagan, beating drums of savages, which, to Native

Americans, was a spiritual and soothing vibration, simulating the heartbeat of the Mother!

Is it any wonder that there similarly is a vast discrepancy in Ray systems, and understanding them becomes extremely confusing for the beginning Ascended Master student?

Ray Systems

Most Ascended Master teachings contain varying information on the Rays. There are a variety of books written on Ascended Master Ray Systems, and I recommend any book written by Alice Bailey. My favorite source book on the *Rays is Law of Life, Volume Two* by A. D. K. Luk. This popular series of books, known by many as the "Yellow Books," was written by the former secretary to Guy Ballard. (Guy and Edna Ballard are the founders of the I AM Activity from which the famous "Green Books" were published.) This volume features a wonderful pull-out Ray Scheme on page 382, giving various attributes and features.

Most classic Ray Systems offer Seven Rays total in defining energy types—which I would recommend for beginning students. However, I have seen systems offering as many as forty different energy types.

To understand differing Ray Systems from diverse Ascended Master sources, focus on the color (as physical light) and throw away the numbering systems. Through this methodology the Pink Ray's attributes are always clearly shown and not confused by numerical order; similarly, the Yellow Ray's attributes come shining through (no pun intended) and confusion about order is eliminated.

Below is a Ray System that I have compiled using Ascended Master teachings and Jyotish (Vedic Astrology) laws. Interestingly, Jyotish means, "Science of Light." I have incorporated the Vedic System alongside the Ascended Master teachings for two reasons: (1) Vedic is the oldest system containing information on Ray Forces that is available on Earth. Since its roots trace back to 4000 BC, it has stood the test of time. (2) In practice and theory, this combination works; the systems are completely similar and compatible, so it is highly likely that the Vedic System was the system studied by many of the Master Teachers: Sananda, Saint Germain, El Morya, Kuthumi, Buddha, etc.

There are two levels of attributes given. Common qualities and cosmic qualities and a planet are identified with each Ray Force. Planets and Ray Forces are key in understanding how Ray Forces work in our solar system.

Blue Ray
Common Attributes: Steady; calm; persevering; transforming; harmonizing; diligent; determined; austere; protective; humble; truthful; self-negating; stern. Cosmic Attribute: Divine Will or Choice. Planet: Saturn.

Yellow Ray
Common Attributes: Studious; learned; expansive; optimistic; joyful; fun-loving; generous; proper; formal. Cosmic Attribute: Spiritual Enlightenment. Planet: Jupiter.

Pink Ray
Common Attributes: Loving; nurturing; hopeful; heartfelt; compassionate; considerate; communicative; intuitive; friendly; humane; tolerant; adoring. Cosmic Attribute: Divine Mother. Planet: Moon.

White Ray
Common Attributes: Beautiful; pure; elegant; refined; sensitive; charming; graceful; creative; artistic; cooperative; uplifting; strong; piercing; blissful. Cosmic Attribute: Divine Feminine. Planet: Venus.

Green Ray
Common Attributes: Educated; thoughtful; communicative; organized; intellectual; objective; scientific; discriminating; practical; discerning; adaptable; rational; healing; awakened. Cosmic Attribute: Active Intelligence. Planet: Mercury.

Ruby and Gold Ray
Ruby—Common Attributes: Energetic; passionate; devoted; determination; dutiful; dependable; direct; insightful; inventive; technical; skilled; forceful. Cosmic Attribute: Divine Masculine. Planet: Mars.

Gold Ray

Common Attributes: Warm; perceptive; honest; confident; positive; independent; courageous; enduring; vital; leadership; responsible; ministration; authority; justice. Cosmic Attribute: Divine Father. Planet: Sun.

Violet Ray

Common Attributes: Forgiving; transmuting; alchemizing; electric; intervening; diplomatic; magical; merciful; graceful; freedom; ordered service. Cosmic Attribute: Divine Grace. Planet: Currently undetermined but some systems place Uranus and/or the higher Vibration of Saturn under this Ray Force.

Co-Creation through the Rays: Gemstones, Mantras, Decrees, and Aromatherapy

Working with the Rays for spiritual growth and evolution opens the soul to the process of Co-Creation. When you begin to access the pure, restorative energy of each Ray Force, many changes will begin in your life. Sometimes, the changes are subtle and take time and perseverance. But often they are immediate and the added support from the Ray brings healing to many aspects of a person's life: relationship, career, money, and health. At a spiritual level, working with the Rays improves and sharpens the super-senses. Many people have reported enhanced psychic and telepathic links with Master Teachers after Mantra and/or Decree work. Mantras and Decrees for the Rays performed in groups are very healing and produce the Fifth Dimensional energies of collective consciousness, Oneship, or what the Ascended Masters call, Unana.

Gemstones are one of the simplest and most effective ways to correct Ray deficiencies or to enhance and intensify the attributes of a Ray. You can wear the gemstone so it touches the skin (this is classic in Jyotish) or you can hold a cluster of crystals to intensify a Ray Force while you meditate. You may also use a gemstone elixir for extra support. Remember that it is best to use a gemstone that is not dyed or heat-treated. (Unfortunately, today, many are.) So check before you begin to use a gemstone for spiritual purposes. Below is a table listing Ray Forces contained in precious gemstones. There are many other tables and information on the esoteric Ray qualities found in semi-precious gemstones; this is a just a simple guideline.

Blue Ray: Blue sapphire and blue topaz. Lap...

Yellow Ray: Yellow sapphire and yellow topaz. Citri...

Pink Ray: Pearl and moonstone. Pink tourmaline gives good results. The best metal for the energies of the Moon, Divine Mother, is silver.

White Ray: Diamond and white sapphire. Very clear, high quality quartz crystal works well.

Green Ray: Emerald and green tourmaline. Green peridot works well too.

Ruby and Gold Ray: Ruby Ray: Red coral. Gold Ray: Red ruby and red garnet are good gemstones for the energies of the sun, Divine Father. Good metals are yellow and white gold.

Violet Ray: Amethyst is best, however I have seen good results with purple sugilite.

Since light and sound function as twins, the importance of understanding the dual functioning of Rays cannot be overlooked or understated. In a recent discourse on Ray Forces taught by El Morya, the Master Teacher of the Blue Ray articulates, "Now understand, Dear ones, chelas, that even sound itself works as a Ray. It is through this circular vibration, which we have explained before as the spiral, that light and sound join to one another."[34] Mantras invoke the energy of a Ray Force with scientific precision. Dr. David Frawley, an authority on Vedic and Hindu spiritual tradition writes, "Mantras are seed sounds (the foremost of which is Om) that contain the laws and the archetypes behind all the workings of energy in the universe. Applying this mantric knowledge on different levels, any domain of existence can be comprehended in its inner truth. Through the mantra, the Rishis were able to be adept in all fields of knowledge, including Yoga, philosophy, astrology, geomancy, medicine, poetry, art, and music. This root knowledge

...rument on which all knowledge can be
...les."[35]

...it with the bija (which means "one") seed
...y chanting Om, place your forefinger and
...ones. You should feel a vibration through your
...ing within your skull. This vibration affects your
...s your entire Chakra System. Inevitably, this sound vibra-
...orts the light vibration and will appear in your light field, or
aura. I once prescribed a Ruby Ray mantra for a client. She ardently
chanted before sitting for a kirlian photographer. To her amazement,
her auric photograph came back filled with red and ruby light! Here is a
chart of the classic bija seed mantras for each of the Rays.

> Blue Ray: Om Sham or Om Shanti
> Yellow Ray: Om Gum
> Pink Ray: Om Som
> White Ray: Om Shum
> Green Ray: Om Bum
> Ruby Ray: Om Ung
> Gold Ray: Om Sum
> Violet Ray: Om Hue

Decrees are another form of working with the Rays and their
energies. Violet Flame decrees are used worldwide by thousands of
Ascended Master students. They can be spoken individually or used in
groups to generate the benefits of the Violet Ray: mercy, compassion,
and forgiveness. One of my favorite decrees is the simple Violet Fire
decree by Mark Prophet, "I AM a being of Violet Fire! I AM the purity
God desires!" Decrees or mantras are often said rhythmically, in groups
of seven or in rounds of 108. (e.g., using a mala, similar to a Catho-
lic Rosary.) Decrees and mantras can also be repeated silently in your
mind, similar to a prayer, in preparation for meditation. El Morya lends
further insight: "And it is when this is consciously applied by the chela,
through the work of the Violet Flame or other mantra work that they
may engage in, that light is then bonded to sound. For ultimately this
is the intertwining of consciousness with action." Simply stated, sound
activates light and together they command the Ray Force into conscious
activity.

The Scent of a Ray

Certain scents also contain the essence of a Ray Force. Often, before the appearance of an Ascended Being or Angel, a fragrance will frequently imbue the area. Since these highly evolved, spiritual beings have focused their energies upon certain, specific Ray energies, the scent carries the same Vibration of the Ray, much in the same way as light or sound. Very often this aroma holds a healing energy or heightens the energies in the room for the appearance of the Master Teacher. This explains appearances of Mother Mary often accompanied by the strong scent of roses, or Kuan Yin's scent of neroli, (orange blossom). Saint Germain often leaves a fragrance of lavender.

Today it is popular to burn certain incenses and smudge a room with sage to purify the energies. These traditions that have come from shamans and different religious ceremonies are also enhancing and reinforcing Ray energies! Here are some aromas associated with Ray Forces.

Blue Ray: Myrrh, Frankincense, Cedar, and Juniper.
Yellow Ray: Sandlewood and Lotus.
Pink Ray: Jasmine and Gardenia.
White Ray: Rose and Nag Champa.
Green Ray: Mint, Wintergreen. [Sage is also good for the
   Green Ray; it also vibrates to the Gold (Sun) Ray.]
Ruby Ray: Musk and Camphor.
Gold Ray: Ginger and Cinnamon.
Violet Ray: Lavender and Lilac.

The Great Central Sun and Movement of the Rays

In Ascended Master teachings, the energies of Rays originate from The Great Central Sun. This is a larger sun that exists away from our solar system. It is a Master intelligence, and through it the Rays are sent to Earth and mankind is educated and perfected through their influence. The same premise is addressed in Hindu Astrology, however this great sun is known as The Galactic Center. It is known as Brahma, which means creative force or the navel of Vishnu. "From The Galactic Sun emanates the light which determines life and intelligence on Earth and which direct the play of the Seven Rays of Creation and the distribution of Karma."[36]

In the Vedic tradition, the energies of the Galactic Center are transmitted to our solar system by the planet Jupiter. Mars initiates the Ray Force energy and the sun then stabilizes the Rays.

According to Ascended Master Teachings, Ray Forces enter our solar system by emanation to our sun. (Hence, the use of Om before each bija seed mantra.) Ray Forces move by two principles: emanation and radiation. From the sun, the energies radiate to the core of the Earth. From the center of the Earth's core, Ray Forces emanate to the Earth's surface. Emanation means to flow out, issue, or proceed as from a source or origin. Radiation is defined as the emission and diffusion of Rays of heat, light, electricity, or sounds. When we personally apply the energies of the Rays through gemstones, mantras, and scents, we are utilizing the second principle of Ray movement, radiation.

Archangels, Ascended Masters, and Ray Forces

All Ascended Beings and Archetypes of Evolution have applied the Rays to achieve higher states of perfection. Through their knowledge of the grand interplay of the Rays, they have overcome karmic reaction and retribution, opened the doors of liberation, and have achieved higher states of consciousness and perfect enlightenment. Each Ascended Master individualizes him/herself upon a Ray Force when in service as a Master Teacher to humanity, and the qualities and attributes of the Masters' teaching will clearly reflect the energies of that particular Ray. Very often before Saint Germain speaks, he will qualify the discourse (teaching) through the Ray Force. A typical greeting is, "I AM Saint Germain, and I stream forth on the Mighty Violet Ray of Mercy, Compassion, and Forgiveness."

Similarly, Archangels also work on a specific, qualified Ray Force. Here are the seven Archangels and the Rays that they represent. Following is a Master Teacher for each Ray Force. (Please note that a Master Teacher may at times work with all Seven Rays to achieve a specific mission. However, it has been noted that certain Master Teachers primarily work with certain Rays and they are often identified with certain Ray Forces; therefore they are listed for single Ray Forces for teaching purposes. However, there are many Master Teachers working on all of the Rays.)

Blue Ray: Archangel Michael. Master Teacher El Morya

Yellow Ray: Archangel Jophiel. Master Teacher Lanto

Pink Ray: Archangel Chamuel. Beloved Mother Mary

Green Ray: Archangel Raphael. Master Teacher Hilarion

White Ray: Archangel Gabriel. Master Teacher Serapis Bey

Ruby and Gold Ray: Archangel Uriel. Master Teacher Kuthumi (Lord Sananda is often identified with this Ray, as well as the Green Ray.)

Violet Ray: Archangel Zadkiel. Master Teacher Saint Germain. (Kuan Yin is often identified with this Ray, as well as the Pink Ray.)

The Esoteric Science behind Chakra and Vortex Systems

Since Ray Forces are present everywhere, their esoteric science is generating and directing all of creation. At the moment of your birth, a snapshot is taken of your astral (light and sound) body. This same information, when converted into the mathematical formulas of Ancient Vedic Rishis, becomes your Rasi, or natal Jyotish (Hindu Astrology) chart. When approached through the language of the Rays, Astrology becomes the logic of the astral body, astral-logic. Each soul chooses the moment of birth so that it has the proper amount of light and sound (the Rays) to fulfill the purpose (dharma) and experiences (karma) of the individual life. The Seven Rays of creation indicate their interplay in every chart, through weaknesses and strengths, manifesting the destiny and actions of the soul. This is why women in childbirth experience short and/or long labors as the soul is picking the perfect moment of birth!

Light and sound is dispersed through the circular movement of the chakras. Clockwise movement indicates a healthy chakra, and it is taking energy in. Counterclockwise movement may indicate disease, or the chakra is removing energies. The septenary order of the Rays is also found in the human energy system; seven chakras and seven layers to the auric field. Each of the seven chakras also relate to each of the Rays. However, in practice, unless the chakras are perfected or balanced, they will emanate many different colors. The table below shows the relationship of the seven chakras to each of the Rays. This segment of information is purely Vedic. (You will note that two Ray Forces identify with the Heart Chakra: the Blue Ray and Pink Ray. These blends of energies depict the perfected state of the heart center—open and receptive (Pink Ray) yet, imbued with the qualities of justice, order, and detachment—the ability to act without bias (Blue Ray).)

Blue Ray: Heart Chakra
Yellow Ray: Third Eye Chakra
Pink Ray: Heart Chakra
White Ray: Sexual Chakra
Green Ray: Throat Chakra
Ruby and Gold Ray: Root Chakra (Ruby) Solar Plexus (Gold)
Violet Ray: Crown Chakra

On Mother Earth, Ray energies are dispersed through the circular movement in a Vortex. Scientifically, a Vortex is a polarized motion body which creates its own magnetic field, aligning molecular structures with phenomenal accuracy. "Nature has basically two types of motion. One is centripetal and the other centrifugal. Those motions have a definite geometrical pattern when they are generated by natural means. This geometrical form is called 'The Vortex.' A Vortex is the three dimensional form by which all mediums like water, air, solids, electricity, magnetism, sound, light, etc. are generally maintained and dissipated. They give birth to and disperse our planet and all particles of matter."[37]

There are many Vortices covering our planet. Some are small and some are very large. Smaller Vortices are classified as either "electrical" or "'magnetic." Yet, all Vortices are electromagnetic and contain many unique energy anomalies. Richard Dannelley, author of *Sedona Power Spot, Vortex and Medicine Wheel Guide* writes, "Their energies affect both our physical and spiritual bodies; expanding the consciousness, and healing the body . . . Vortex energy is sometimes referred to as 'psychic energy.' This is because we know that the electromagnetic Earth energy of the Vortices is capable of stimulating our minds in a manner that triggers 'psychic phenomena,' i.e., events which can be considered to be 'paranormal'—beyond the 'normal' experience of life."[38]

Golden Cities have been discussed numerous times, but we will repeat some of the material for this teaching section of the book:

In the I AM America prophecies, a Golden City Vortex is very unique. In the early work of the late 1980s, Saint Germain described their locations as "Safe Places" before, during, and after Earth Changes. He stated, "These gateways, or Vortex areas are protected areas for interaction with spiritual energy."[39] He also prophesied that after the Earth Changes that Master Teachers would appear in each Golden City Vortex to minister, teach, and heal humanity for a twenty-year period. Then the Earth would enter into a Golden Age of Spiritual Enlightenment, Prosperity, and Peace. Each Golden City Vortex contains individual attributes along with alignment to a Ray energy. In the table that follows are the ten Golden City Vortices for the United States and Canada. In addition to a repetition of earlier material, the year of their activation is listed (this is when the energies are mature enough and developed for use):

Gobean. 1981. El Morya. Arizona/New Mexico. Blue Ray.

Malton. 1994. Kuthumi. Illinois/Indiana. Ruby and Gold Ray.

Wahanee. 1996. Saint Germain. Georgia/S. Carolina. Violet Ray.

Shalahah. 1998. Sananda. Idaho/Montana. Green Ray.

Klehma. 2000. Serapis Bey. Colorado/Kansas. White Ray.

Pashachino. 2002. Soltec. Alberta/British Columbia. Green Ray.

Eabra. 2004. Portia. Yukon/NW Territories. Violet Ray.

Jeafray. 2006. Archangel Zadkiel and Beloved Holy Amethyst. Quebec. Violet Ray.

Uverno. 2008. Paul the Venetian. Manitoba/Ontario. Pink Ray.

Yuthor. 2010. Hilarion. Greenland. Green Ray.

Stienta. 2012. Archangel Michael. Iceland. Blue Ray.

Denasha. 2014. Lady Nada. Scotland. Yellow Ray.

Amerigo. 2016. Godfre. Spain. Gold Ray.

Gruecha. 2018. Hercules. Norway and Sweden. Blue Ray.

Braun. 2020. Victory. Germany, Poland, Czechoslovakia. Yellow Ray.

Afrom. 2022. Claire and SeRay. Hungary and Romania. White Ray.

Ganakra. 2024. Vista. Turkey. Green Ray

Mesotamp. 2026. Mohammed. Turkey, Iran, and Iraq. Yellow Ray.

Shehez. 2028. Tranquility. Iran and Afghanistan. Ruby and Gold Rays.

Adjatal. 2030. Lord Himalayan. Afghanistan, Pakistan, and India. Blue and Gold Rays.

[Editor's Note: For more information on Golden City Vortex Activation Dates, Presiding Ray, and Master Teacher see: *Light of Awakening*, pages 187–197.]

Over the last ten years, the Master Teachers have shared many details concerning the Golden City Vortices and our knowledge has significantly increased on this topic. Since Ray energies emanate from the central core of the Earth to the Earth's surface, the energy of the Ray radiates from the center (apex) of the Vortex and is dispersed through the circular motion as described in chakra energy movement. Therefore the centers of Golden City Vortices, which the Master Teachers call "Stars," are enormously charged with the beneficial Ray energies. Stars are approximately forty miles in diameter, but the high energies can be sensed up to sixty miles. Living in a Star area of a Golden City Vortex will produce self-knowledge and self-empowerment. In the New Times, the Stars of each Golden City Vortex will be used as ceremonial grounds and their energies are good for self-renunciation, meditation, and spiritual liberation.

"As our ears are opened and our eyes begin to see, let us join as ONE LIGHT, in our hearts and minds. May this light of wisdom serve all. May this light of truth and justice prevail. May this law be written in hearts and joined through harmony, Brotherhood, and love.

Timelessly and agelessly, the unknown poet sings, 'O, let not the flame die out! Cherished age after age in its dark cavern—in its holy temples cherished. Fed by pure ministers of love—let not the flame die out!'"

~ Master K.H.[40]

Awakening Prayer

This prayer was given by Ascended Masters Sai
to assist the Cellular Awakening of humanity. I
spoken individually, and used in meditation. 7
duced to over 200 people at the Global Scienc
Colorado, 1990:

Great Light of Divine Wisdom,
Stream forth to my being,
And through your right use
Let me serve mankind and the planet.
Love, from the Heart of God.
Radiate my being with the presence of the Christ
That I walk the path of truth.
Great source of creation.
Empower my being,
my brother,
my sister,
and my planet
with perfection
As we collectively awaken as ONE cell.
I call forth the Cellular Awakening.
Let wisdom, love, and power stream forth to this cell,
This cell that we all share.
Great spark of creation awaken the Divine Plan of Perfection.
So we may share the ONE perfected cell,
I AM.

...editation

...September 11, 2001, the Spiritual Teachers shared their
...garding the shocking, inhumane tragedy. Now with a per-
...e on this event after well over a decade, I have no doubt that
...fficially entered the prophesied "Time of Testing." Voices joined
...ound the globe, repeating a solemn, mourning statement full of a
sense of innocence lost: "The world will never be the same again." And,
indeed, from that moment many events shaped and shifted our en-
trance into a New Time.

Emails poured in to our address from all over the globe. There
were many different perspectives, opinions, good ideas, and sincere
thoughts upon this time in history. One provocative question was: "Are
we at the beginning of a new era—an era that returns to the balance of
the feminine, lest we perish?" A translated prayer sent from our friends
in Switzerland mirrored similar thoughts:

> "We beseech that in all the suffering a truth begin to dawn.
> We beseech for the beginning of a huge, worldwide awakening.
> We pray for an inner, global spirit of reconciliation and insight,
> a spirit to wipe away all our old patterns."

As an old era ended, a New Time commenced for humanity's
spiritual growth and evolution. During the "Time of Testing," the Spiritual Teachers have assured us that we will never be "tested beyond our
abilities."

Peace Is a Choice

Do we accept a world filled with terrorism and the intentional psychic
horror it inflicts upon millions of people? Clarissa Pinkola Estes, PhD,
wrote in an email, "This infection that terrorists hope to circulate is
that of innocent persons becoming afraid of life, afraid of the future; of
causing people to put off the living of life, to move in ways that are far
less than their previous free selves." In any choice or Co-creation process, the Ascended Masters often remind us of the higher intelligence
contained in Universal Laws and their potential to transform lower
frequencies of hatred, violence, and fear into balance, love, and eternal
peace. A good friend emailed the insightful words of Saint Germain
through channel Donna Simelunas: "For every act of darkness and de-

struction there is an opening for an equal constru[...]
Light." Clearly, violence is a choice to destroy. Pea[...]
Several days after the tragedy of 9-11, Saint Germ[...]
shared teachings on building inner peace through [...]
son, "Lighting the Heart of Peace."

    These times have many spiritual students [...]
such events can serve the Divine Plan and Divine [...]
answers through a statement of Hermetic Law: "All comes forward seeking a balance—all extremes finding their other complement." He then offered a healing decree:

> "Mighty Violet Flame, come forth! Stream forth into my will.
> Align my will to the Divine Plan and bring balance to this situation."

The Time of Testing

The Ascended Masters remind us that: "A test is given so one can reevaluate their choices. This test brings about a search for inner peace. Let us find the center of balance, the calm, the inner knowing, and The Divine Will that flows in a harmony and a rhythm." Events of global change and turmoil are only a backdrop for you to search and understand the need for inner peace, the eternal ONE—the Christ Consciousness the Ascended Masters call Unana.

The Consciousness of Unana

Unana is another name for the Unified Field of human consciousness. Major General Kulwant Singh of India explains, "This field of consciousness—termed the unified field in the language of quantum physics—is millions of times more fundamental and powerful than nuclear force."

    The Spiritual Teacher Sananda elaborates, "If you are feeling fear, if you are feeling vengeance, if you are feeling anger toward your Brother, it is important to keep the Flame of Love within your heart. It is important to keep the Light of the Christ Consciousness burning within your rational mind. Open your heart to compassion for the suffering in this Plane of Duality. Apply this higher law to transmute the situation to a higher understanding."

    In India, more than 25,000 meditating experts assembled according to Major Singh, a thirty-five year career army veteran who

this will produce an indomitable influence of peace and
in the country. No nation will ever be moved to attack India,
comes a lighthouse of peace and coherence to its neighbors and
world."

Group Meditation

All spiritual work, primarily prayer and meditation are extremely effective in any Star area of a Golden City Vortex for World Peace. The Ascended Masters' instruction focuses on Lord Sananda's Heart Meditation and recommends that a group of seven focused on this meditation can effect personal change for global peace. When used on a regular basis, the decrees (mantras) will help in the transmutation of the group and the meditation will assist the focus for the fulfillment of peace.

The Golden City Stars—Critical Points

Stars of Golden City Vortices function with unique similarity to a technique developed by David Hawkins while mapping states of human consciousness in his attractor research, known as critical point analysis. In his book *Power Versus Force* he writes of this process, "Critical point analysis is a technique derived from the fact that in any highly complex system there is a specific critical point at which the smallest input will result in the greatest change. The great gears of a windmill can be halted by lightly touching the right escape mechanism; it is possible to paralyze a giant locomotive if you know exactly where to put your finger."[41]

In essence, the critical point of each Golden City Vortex is the Star, (a forty mile radius) where the least amount of force exerts the greatest effect. Towns and cities located in United States Golden City Stars are:

Star of Gobean

Pinetop, AZ

Lakeside, AZ

Springerville, AZ

Eagar, AZ

Star of Malton

Mattoon, IL

Charleston, IL

Shelbyville, IL

Sullivan, IL

Humboldt, IL

Star of Wahanee

Augusta, GA

Grovetown, GA

Appling, GA

Harlem, GA

Gracewood, GA

Thompson, GA

Modeo, GA

North Augusta, SC

Trenton, SC

Eureka, SC

Parksville, SC

Kitchings Mill, SC

Williston, SC

Star of Shalahah

Lolo Pass, MT

Lolo, MT

Missoula, MT

Stevensville, MT

Star of Klehma

Cope, CO

Joes, CO

Kirk, CO

A Decree before the Meditation

It is suggested to use this decree before Sananda's Heart Meditation.

"Mighty Violet Flame blaze forth from the Heart of the Central Sun—leap into my heart and light the Flame of Compassion within me!"

"Mighty Violet Flame, in the name of God that I AM, embrace this entire planet, and flood it with the Light Supreme of the Violet Ray. May the Violet Flame enfold all leadership of this world and align the Harmony of the Spheres through the great Law, I AM. So be it!"

Sananda's Heart Meditation

This is Sananda's instruction: "It is important at this time for those who seek the Christ within, to find it through inner meditation. First, it is important to silence the mind. This may be done with several decrees. Sit in contemplation—gently close the eyes. Focus all energy upon the heart. In that moment of the focus of energy on the heart, feel within the connection to all of life. Feel this heart is connected to all of life—the radiating pulse that is in all living creatures and all living consciousness."

"This consciousness that permeates all living things, is the consciousness of the ONE—Unana. Meditate upon this pulse, work to hear this pulse within the inner ear. In this inner hearing comes a radiation. This radiation is the growth of a new energy body. This energy source is carried with you throughout the day. Bless all that you come in contact with through the day. Carry the radiance of this loving Christ throughout your day. This I encourage all to do. Focus in the mind upon the colors of white and gold. This will bring about a calming and a healing effect upon the consciousness—it also brings about unification of the self. So be it."

eage of the Violet Flame

gs of the Violet Flame, as taught in the work of I AM
come through the Goddess of Compassion and Mercy, Kuan
e holds the feminine aspects of the Flame, which are compas-
mercy, forgiveness, and peace. Her work with the Violet Flame is
ll documented in the history of Ascended Master Teachings, and it
s said that the altar of the etheric Temple of Mercy holds the Flame in
a lotus cup. She became Saint Germain's teacher of the Sacred Fire in
the inner realms, and he carried the masculine aspect of the Flame into
human activity through purification, alchemy, and transmutation. One
of the best means to attract the beneficent activities of the Violet Flame
is through the use of decrees and invocation. However, you can meditate upon and visualize the Flame and receive its transmuting energies
like "the light of a thousand suns," radiant and vibrant as the first day
that the Elohim Arcturus and Diana drew it forth from our solar Sun at
the Creation of the Earth. Whatever form, each time you use the Violet
Flame, these two Master Teachers hold you in the loving arms of its action and power.

Following is an invocation for the Violet Flame to be used at
sunrise or sunset. It is utilized while experiencing the visible change of
night to day, and day to night. In fact, if you observe the horizon at
these times, you will witness light transitioning from pinks to blues, and
then a subtle violet strip adorns the sky. We have used this invocation
for years in varying scenes and circumstances, overlooking lakes, rivers,
mountaintops, deserts and prairies, in huddled traffic and busy streets,
with groups of students or sitting with a friend, but more commonly
alone in our home or office, with a glint of soft light streaming from a
window. The result is always the same: a calm, centering force of stillness. We call it *the Space*.

Invocation of the Violet Flame for Sunrise and Sunset
I invoke the Violet Flame to come forth in the name of I AM
That I AM,
To the Creative Force of all the realms of all the Universes, the
Alpha, the Omega, the Beginning and the End,
To the Great Cosmic Beings and Torch Bearers of all the realms
of all the Universes,

And the Brotherhoods and Sisterhoods of Breath, Sound and Light, who honor this Violet Flame that comes forth from the Ray of Divine Love—the Pink Ray, and the Ray of Divine Will—the Blue Ray of all Eternal Truths.

I invoke the Violet Flame to come forth in the name of I AM That I AM!

Mighty Violet Flame, Stream forth from the Heart of the Central Logos, the Mighty Great Central Sun! Stream in, through, and around me.

(Then insert other prayers and/or decrees for the Violet Flame.)

Science of Light

As mentioned earlier, Jyotish, or the "Science of Light," is also the intricate personal science of the Seven Rays of Light and Sound. The Grahas (*graha* is Sanskrit for planet) weave a web of light and sound upon us at the moment of our first breath into our earthly bodies. Under the spell of this web of illusion, we are prisoners and held captive in the field of actions, bound to cycles of rebirth, karma (action), and dharma (purpose).

Jyotish was given to humanity before consciousness fell into the dark cycle of time, Kali Yuga. Its origin is traced to the Vedic Rishis (advanced spiritual teachers who lived in the previous ages of superior light and truth at the beginning of this cycle of human civilization) and seer Parashara Shakti and his great work, Brihat Parashara Hora Shastra. Through understanding and applying this profound system, we reintegrate and Master the light and sound of the Grahas, and their Cup pours spiritual light that illumines our life's journey to spiritual freedom and Ascension.

Jyotish is based upon the Sidereal Zodiac, which corresponds to actual constellations and the fixed locations of the stars in the sky. Its Zodiac also orients to a central galactic sun, known as The Galactic Center and it takes approximately 25,000 years for the Earth to make a full circuit. The famed psychic Edgar Cayce used a sidereal system, and predicted that it would prevail over time. According to Dr. David Frawley, "Vedic astrology has existed over many thousands of years. A number of changes of equinoctial positions similar to our Age of Aquarius and similar shifts in the calendar have been recorded in it. The Vedic system and its zodiac are based upon a continuity of culture that goes back to the Age of the Gods when human beings still had communication with the intelligence of the cosmos." [42]

The Nine Grahas and Their Mantras

Graha means, "to grab" or "to hold," and according to the Vedic Rishis a Graha has the ability to grasp our consciousness in a veil of hypnosis. Perhaps this is why another one of the meanings of Graha is "demon" or "what possesses a person." Yet another lighter meaning of Graha is simply "cup." It appears that there are two viewpoints on the planetary forces: one entirely structures and forms our thoughts, feelings, and actions; another pours light upon our lives, lifting and redeeming us to higher levels of enlightenment. As in most spiritual sciences, the nine planets of astrology mirror our evolutionary path on Earth and show the powerful metaphor of choice resurrecting us out of darkness into self-knowledge, life, and light.

According to the Vedic Rishis, each of the planets makes a basic sound frequency. This teaching becomes the basis of the *bija-* (one) syllable mantra. (A mantra is a sound or vibration used in meditation and devotional ceremonies in order to produce higher states of consciousness.) I have listed the bija seed mantras for the Rays. Here are the bija seed mantras for the nine Grahas:

☉**SUN:** Om Sum, pronounced "soom." (The Divine Father)

☽**MOON:** Om Som. (The Divine Mother)

♂**MARS:** Om Am, pronounced "ung." (Divine Masculine or Action)

☿**MERCURY:** Om Bum, pronounced "boom." (Divine Intelligence)

♃**JUPITER:** Om Gum, pronounced "goom." (Divine Guru or Teacher)

♀**VENUS:** Om Shum. (Divine Feminine or Beauty)

♄**SATURN:** Om Sham. (Divine Forgiveness or Peace)

☊**RAHU:** Om Rahm. (Divine Help and Protection)

☋**KETU:** Om Kem, pronounced "kehm." (Divine Awareness)

The Art of Channeling

It was the third time that I had interviewed on the national radio late-night talk show. The interviewer was perceptive and to the point: "I'm sorry, Lori, I just don't find channeled information credible." For the last ten years "trance channel" would have best described my career. And now, seventeen million avid listeners had heard that their beloved host did not find my information believable. I understood perfectly why a remark like this was common; it was a concern that I had heard many times before. I kept quiet and waited for the next caller; but my heart burned with the truth. I knew he was wrong.

The same experience, to some extent happened in another media interview when I inadvertently used the word "channel" to explain the source of my information. "Oh no, we can't use that word, it will incite far too much. Is there another word that you could use?" interrupted the host. We settled on the phrase "meditative state."

Several years ago in one of my "meditative states," Ascended Master Sananda gave an insightful teaching: "I have no more divinity than you," he said. "And you have no more than I. What is the difference? The difference is the experience." Then his normally calm and balanced state lit up and inferred a state of spiritual ecstasy on me.

Inspiration through spiritual experience is similarly documented in stories about the 525 BC Indian Prince Siddhartha. The wealthy son of a king near present-day Nepal had been six years in his constant search for the truth, and his body was broken and weak from constant wandering and the practice of extreme austerities. Through the aid of local villagers, he began to eat and slowly he regained his health. When he resumed his search, he discovered that he had prayed at every shrine and there was nowhere left to go. Spirits danced about him as he sat underneath the Banyan tree and a voice said, "Give it up, it is of no use. Go back to the pleasures you have left behind." Discouraged and weary, the mind of the prince went inward and suddenly he floated above the tree and into every corner of the Earth. "He saw men being born, he saw them suffering and dying, and he followed their souls around the mysterious cycle of rebirth until he saw them return again to the Earth. The prince seemed to walk within the very hearts of men until he knew all their dreamings, yearnings and longings." [43] His consciousness ascended to yet another level and there he encountered supernatural beings, sages, and spiritual teachers that dwelt in the divine, heavenly worlds. His consciousness returned to the Banyan Tree and he opened his eyes to be greeted by hundreds of monks, sages, and saints walking out of the skies, welcoming him and accepting him into their order. This meditative state experience became a point of departure for the prince who became the twenty-ninth Enlightened One, known as Buddha. Refusing to leave this Earth for the Heavens of Nirvana, Buddha stayed on for forty-five more years to teach and to help others. Today it is estimated that there are over 300 million followers of Buddhism.

When Buddha graced this Earth with his presence, did he ever channel his teachings to his students? Most likely. The word channel makes some folks' teeth itch. But the truth is that this experience or a form of it is a common thread in many religions.

Muslims, Quakers, and Mormons: a Common Thread
When Muhammad visited a cave in 610 AD on Mount Hira outside of Mecca, he had a vision and a message given to him by God. This experience continued throughout his life and the revelations contained in these visions constitute the text of the Koran.

In 1652, George Fox began preaching in Puritan England that there was "that of God in every man." His movement, based upon religious tolerance and an inward experience of God, became known as The Society of Friends, commonly called Quakers. They hold that believers receive Divine Guidance from an Inner Light, without the aid of intermediaries or external rites.[44] Groups of Quakers immigrated to colonial America and, following leader William Penn, founded in Pennsylvania a refuge as a "holy experiment" in religious tolerance. They raised their political voice in a number of reforms including: anti-slavery, Indian rights, prison reform, and the women's movement.

Joseph Smith was directed by heavenly messengers when he found ancient gold plates inscribed in a hieroglyphic language in 1830. Since he had been visited by Jesus and other heavenly beings four years earlier in a vision warning him not to join any of the existing churches in his hometown of Palmyra, New York, and prophesying that his life work was to establish the restored Christian church, his translation of the gold plates was most likely divinely inspired. Through his translation, the plates told the history about an ancient group of people who migrated from Jerusalem to America around 600 BC to 421 AD. He also translated the religious beliefs of these people into the Book of

Mormon. Today, Mormons believe that God continues to reveal his word, primarily to leaders of local units and to the President-Prophet for the church as a whole.[45]

So again, I ask, "Were these spirit-led founders of different religions channeling?" Probably. But please, read on and make your own decision.

A Definition of Channel

A few traditional definitions of the word channel are:

1. A frequency band wide enough for one-way communication, the exact width of a channel depending upon the type of transmission involved (as telegraph, telephone, radio, television, etc.)

2. A groove or furrow.

3. A route through which anything passes.

4. To direct toward or into some particular course: to channel one's interests.[46]

I kind of like the idea that channeling could be defined as a spiritual groove. Through my experience, I propose yet another definition for a channeler: Spiritual Artist. In the free-flowing and uncharted waters of the super-conscious, the channel paints an individual image of an experience with the Divine. Each word becomes a delicate brush stroke; universal ideas and truths present shadows, light, depth, and dimension; and the whole thing is colored with the hues and tones of beliefs and experiences. Joseph Campbell gives the poet of consciousness the highest compliment: "They come from an elite experience, the experience of people particularly gifted, whose ears are open to the song of the universe." [47]

Shamanism and Native American Culture

Native American cultures understood, valued, and respected this state of consciousness. They knew that it was a talent, a gift. When the Sioux spiritualist Black Elk was nine years old, he became sick, psychologically. The boy was completely immobilized, trembled, and began to see deities. His parents quickly summoned a shaman. Instead of casting out the offensive demon, the shaman worked to adapt Black Elk to the deities and the deities to Black Elk. The nine-year-old boy went on to become a spiritual leader and prophet for his tribe. The German philosopher Freidrich Nietzsche once said, "Be careful lest in casting out the devils you cast out the best thing that's in you." Indigenous cultures from South America to Siberia regarded and valued the talents of the one who could cross the threshold of this world and open up another. In *The Power of Myth*, Joseph Campbell speaks about the shaman: "The shaman is the person, male or female, who in his late childhood or early youth has an overwhelming psychological experience that runs him totally inward. It's a kind of schizophrenic crack-up. The whole unconscious opens up, and the shaman falls into it." [48] From my work as a trance channel, I understand this statement.

Channeling was very common with the Pawnees and their priest was considered to be a medium of communication with their Spiritual Teacher, Ti-ra-wa. Often he would act as an intercessor for the tribe and, through his instruction from Ti-ra-wa, he was given specific training on the secrets of the sacred bundles. His prayers and requests for his tribe or for an individual were often granted because "his education and the power given him from above brought him into specially close relations with Ti-ra-wa, who seemed to watch over him . . . He was an intermediary between Ti-ra-wa and the people, and held a relation to the Pawnees and their deity not unlike that occupied by Moses to Jehovah and the Israelites." [49]

Ancient Hindu Signs of the Talent

The Vedic astrologers of ancient India whose art developed thousands of years ago knew that this gift existed and gave clues of how to recognize if a person would or could become a channel through certain astrological configurations. Ketu, which is the Sanskrit name for the Moon's south node, is also known as the *moksha karaka*, which means "indicator of enlightenment." A pronounced Ketu in an Eastern Indian (sidereal) chart indicates one who is a spiritual seeker with great powers of discrimination, other-worldliness, detachment from this world, and sometimes psychic ability. When the Sun or the Moon is conjoined with Ketu, the meaning of this force is further increased and metaphysical, spiritual, and psychic tendencies flourish. Today, this conjunction is known by Vedic astrologers to be present in the charts of professional psychics. [50]

Different Methods of Channeling

The methodology of a channel can vary depending on the disposition, ability, and experience of the individual. When I first became acquainted with channeling, I had the opportunity to experience in person a number of channels. They were all very different and while their information and methodologies varied, they all exhibited altered states of consciousness.

One said a prayer prior to her work that she claimed, "Always put her into a trance." Another spoke in a completely altered voice: harsh and raspy, like an old man. The channel herself was around fifty-plus, had two grown children, and her retired husband managed her readings. She sat upright in a chair as she gave the reading, and the channeled entity waved a pointed finger at me.

I met a very unusual channel in Phoenix, Arizona. This channel walked around and examined some fifty of us before the channeling for all of us began. My most profound experience during this time was with a channel in Salt Lake City. This channel sat on a stage in full-body trance. The entity used the body with great comfort and sat like a wise old king, one leg crossed over the other. One hand cradled an elbow and the free hand steadily rubbed an invisible beard. The energy was incredible, the information lucid, understandable, and impactful.

An acquaintance of mine works as a channel. Her relationship with her Spiritual Teacher had been long for channeling—around fifteen years. Her style is very integrative and she remains approachable; no extreme trance, but more of an inner dialogue with her mentor. Her voice remains quite normal; the information is perceptive and somewhat psychic.

Visits and Meetings with Spiritual Teachers

Many channels report that before their work as a channel begins, they are often visited in physical form by their Spiritual Teachers. This was true of Helena Blavatsky, an incredibly gifted psychic and medium who co-founded The Theosophical Society in 1875. In an 1887 meeting she spoke of her Master Teacher: "I met him first when I was twenty—in 1851. He was in the very prime of manhood then. I am an old woman now, but he has not aged a day."[51]

In 1895, when Alice Bailey was fifteen years old, she sat alone on Sunday morning in her drawing room reading. The door opened and in walked a tall man dressed in European clothes with a turban on his head. He told the impetuous teenager that there was some work planned for her to do, but it would entail changing her disposition considerably. She was told, "My future usefulness to Him and to the world was dependent upon how I handled myself and the changes I could manage to make."[52] Twenty years later, she reflected on that life-changing meeting, "I found that this visitor was the Master Koot Hoomi, a Master who is very close to the Christ . . . The real value of this experience is not to be found in the fact that I, a young girl called Alice La Trobe-Bateman, had an interview with a Master but in the fact that knowing nothing whatsoever of their existence, I met one of Them and that He talked with me."[53] Alice Bailey worked for over fifty years as a channel for her Spiritual Teachers. During this time she wrote and published twenty-four books and founded a school based on the teachings that she dictated.

Edgar Cayce, famous for channeling diagnostic and health information in over 14,000 readings and founding the Association for Research and Enlightenment in 1934, was just thirteen years old when a woman appeared to him while he was sitting in the woods on a pleasant May afternoon in Hopkinsville, Kentucky. At first he thought the woman was his mother but then she spoke in a pure, ethereal voice: "Your prayers have been heard. Tell me what you would like most of all, so that I may give it to you." The young Edgar replied, "Most of all I would like to be helpful to others, especially to children when they are sick."[54]

Sometimes introductory meetings between potential Spiritual Teachers and channels do not happen in the physical. One channel shared her story with me: "I was not the type of person who believed in channeling; in fact I thought it was a bunch of nonsense! I was a student of spiritual material and invited the Christ Consciousness into my heart. Things changed after that and I started on a path of spiritual awakening and unfoldment. I attended spiritual healing and meditation classes; I studied and became a hypnotherapist. Several psychic friends started to notice that there was a person (in spirit) around me all of the time. Evidently there was a light, shaped like a tetrahedron about his head. He carried much light in colors of white, gold, and purple. A psychic artist drew a picture of the spirit being for me and told me that his name was Bishop. I thought that was an odd name. Several weeks later, around three in the morning, a loud voice woke me from my sleep: "It is time to write." I knew it was Bishop. I was still very skeptical about this type of information and told him that he would have to wait—but later that day I dictated my first session with Bishop; it was exactly thirteen pages long! A lot of the information was very new to me and taught me a different perspective. There were so many things I had not even thought about! That winter I planted white tulips and in the spring they all came up beautiful and white, except one, it was purple! I know that purple tulip was from Bishop. Even today, and especially when I'm channeling, people will comment about all the purple light around me."

Learning the Ropes

When I began to channel, I didn't know that I was. It sounds funny to say that now, but that was how it started. I had begun meditating in my late teens but it wasn't until I had become an Ascended Master student that I recognized several of the Ascended Masters as my Spiritual Teachers. Often they would appear in my meditation and offer supplemental information to my current studies. This early relationship offered nothing profound for humanity, but for me this help was immensely beneficial, insightful, and broadening. My sessions resembled those between a tutor and student. During this time I met a remarkable woman who became another teacher to me. Leona was well versed in metaphysics and taught me past life regression techniques. She would drive twelve miles out across the Idaho prairie on gravel roads to our remote farm and help get my three preschoolers down for their naps. Then the afternoon was ours! We'd practice the technique and regress one another. Leona was an avid journal keeper and she encouraged me to keep notes of my regressions and of my dreams. I spent an entire year reviewing past lives and in meditation with the help of my Spiritual Teachers was able to understand the significance of each lifetime and its relationship to my current life.

A Meetin[g]

I was alone on a [...]
the barn. I said a[...]
them in some sm[...]
from my sleep. T[...]
before a thunders[...]
main! His aura cr[...]
to touch him and[...]

Five year[s...]
tion and alternati[...]
of us were exchan[...]
my inner instruct[...]
a common occurr[...]
meditating, receiv[...]
laughingly remark[...]
ed that I could ch[...]
with me, I felt ver[...]

for about twenty sessions. Then I began to no[...]
first thing was that I had dropped over ten[...]
Of course this made me quite happy an[...]
sudden weight loss and/or weight ga[...]
nels and particularly when they a[...]
next thing that I noticed was[...]
nagging cough in my thro[...]
System was in the proc[...]
Teachers in preparat[...]
a common story[...]
channeling, a[...]
first book [...]

Spiritual Teachers had been private; sacred. Now, someone else would be included in my time with them, and I felt unsure and insecure. The first couple of sessions were slow and tedious. I was self-conscious and my lack of confidence made it even harder to slip into the familiar, relaxed state of meditation that I knew would be required. At one point we even tried playing soft music, but nothing worked.

Finally, out of frustration I lay down on the couch hoping that I could fall into a light sleep. I had been able to do this before with great success. I closed my eyes and focused my energy and thoughts to the center of my forehead. Soon, thousands of bright lights were rushing at me, a sign of altered consciousness. In about a minute I lifted my hand, "I'm here and they are here."

Physical Changes

In the beginning of my channeling career, the best analogy to describe my methodology was a telephone; better yet, a telephone line. The Spiritual Teachers would telepathically transmit information that I would audibly repeat. A question from my monitor would be asked, and then I would telepathically relay the monitor's question to the Spiritual Teacher and their telepathic answer would be given to me. I would then audibly repeat the answer and so on. This process continued

...ice physical changes. The
...pounds, almost effortlessly.
...d I have since discovered that
...n is typical among trance chan-
...e doing a lot of trance work. The
...a tremendous burning in my chest and a
...t. Later, I discovered that my entire Chakra
...ss of being cleared and purified by my Spiritual
...ion for the work that they had planned. This is also
...mong channels. The entire story of how I opened to
...d received the I AM America Map is recounted in the
...f the I AM America Trilogy, *A Teacher Appears*.

Where Two or More Are Gathered

...most every trance channel works with at least one other person who
is present at every session. The exception to this may be channels who
work via automatic writing or dictation. There are many advantages to
this relationship and while it would appear that the person not channeling is only operating the tape recorder, they are doing much more.

This person performs a very valuable role for the channel; they
become a battery of energy, which assists the channel while in a trance
session. The monitor serves as a source of energy as the channel enters
into trance and becomes a grounding influence after the channel awakes
from the trance state. Therefore, during the trance session, the energy of
the channel and monitor become ONE. You might remember Matthew
18:20, "For where two or three have gathered together in My name,
there I AM in their midst." While it is still possible for a channel to
enter a trance without the help of a monitor, the extra energy provided
by the monitor is extremely helpful.

The monitor can play an important role determining the type
of information that is given. Because the monitor dialogues extensively
with the Spiritual Teacher(s) during each session, the types of questions
asked can sometimes result in new and thought-provoking information. Paul Solomon, a clairvoyant and clairaudient since the age of four
who became a world-renowned deep-trance channeler of the Spiritual
Teacher called simply The Source, learned more about the art of channeling as he and his monitor Harry were told that, "They (the Source)
would not answer any but specific questions; that it was in the framing

and the asking of the question that the response was formulated. So, in order to bait and hook that submarine body of truths they were trying to fish up, Paul and Harry asked what they conceived to be the ultimate specific question—"What is God?"—hoping to elicit some sort of encyclopedic contribution to mankind's store of theological understanding. To their utter bewilderment, the Source replied, simply, God is a being who can recognize good without evil as a point of reference."[55]

    I once spent an entire summer channeling with a new monitor. I've published this story and all of the information that we received in the second book of the I AM America Trilogy – *Sisters of the Flame*. I had been experimenting with sitting up for my trance sessions but still found it difficult to achieve the deeper trance that I was accustomed to. My new monitor, Sherry Takala, encouraged this process and her helpful support allowed my channeling technique to expand and mature. Our sessions were held at her home, which was inordinately alive with frequent visitors in and out of the door, pets running and jumping, constant telephone ringing, and a shortwave radio which was on most of the time. One might think that this would be a difficult environment to channel in, let alone relax! But it was through these adverse conditions that my new abilities were exercised and strengthened. Harry, her affectionate and friendly dog, loved the Spiritual Teachers, and the moment that they would enter via my trance state, he had to say hello. He'd run over, jump on me, and lick my face jarring me from my trance! Sherry would scold him, I'd adjust myself for another try, but often the same thing would happen again. It didn't help much to put him outside. He'd bark until he was let back in. I persevered and soon learned that I could adjust and strengthen my trance state through many types of interference. This little white dog became my teacher of focus and discipline—an important point in channeling. A Spiritual Teacher once said, "Adepts adapt."

    During this time I began to channel for small groups of people. Through this experience I became acquainted with many new subtleties of energy while channeling. If the energy of the group was high and positive, after the session I would feel balanced and energetic. But, if there were negative thoughts or feelings, skepticism or doubt, I would often feel drained and tired. A frequent guest and friend was an enormous battery of energy; I loved for her to sit next to me during these sessions. Her positive energy would embrace me while I was in trance and afterwards I felt physically regenerated. These small nuances can make a large difference for a channel.

Monitors can also work long distance. Twenty years ago I was working on a series of channeled lessons for a Spiritual Teacher. These lessons would be telepathically dictated and written, without the need for tape recorded, voice-received information. I mentioned this to a friend who was also a student of the Ascended Masters and she volunteered to work as my monitor. When I explained to her that the sessions would begin at four thirty A.M. every morning, she didn't hesitate at all, amiably adding, "I'm up anyway at that time." The interesting point is that she lived over 100 miles away and her monitoring would be done through meditation. One morning I slept in and around seven A.M. the phone rang. "Where were you?" she exclaimed. At that moment I realized that the interconnectedness and ONENESS of the channel and monitor could defy physical proximity and location. Almost every trance channel I know works with a monitor and is grateful for their service. Sometimes a channel may work with more than one monitor. Edgar Cayce was said to have worked with two to three.

The Different Levels of Trance

In my early days of navigating the ethereal world, it was near the end of one session when something memorable occurred. I experienced an incredibly high-pitch sound and almost simultaneously an internal explosion of light and consciousness. My voice boomed into the recorder, "I AM Lady Opportunity. May I help you?" Even though I was in a trance state, the feeling jarred me, and I immediately reverted back to the normal session style of relaying questions and answers. After the session, my monitor was grinning from ear to ear. I begged him to play the tape back, so I could hear it again. It was unmistakable; my trance work was evolving.

Through the years of working and learning as a channel, I have come to understand that there are different levels of trance work. While it seems to have little impact on the quality or quantity of information; the depth of the trance seems to be geared for the channel, the monitor, and the degree of work or service that they are performing.

Some channels enter into trances so deep that they have no recall whatsoever of what is being said. They have to listen to or read their own information after the session. This was the type of trance that "The

Sleeping Prophet," Edgar Cayce used. Psychologist Gina Cerminara writes in the book *Many Mansions*, "In his early years Edgar Cayce was as startled as the next man to learn he had given medical counsel to an Italian in fluent and flawless Italian. Nor was the complicated medical terminology that rolled off his tongue any more intelligible to him in his waking state than was the fluent Italian." [56] One time a deep trance channel told me that she would be sent to another place to receive her own instruction as the Spiritual Teacher used her body for its work here. Many trance channels enter into very light trances and are able to remember much of what was transmitted. One of the old arguments against channeling is that deep trances are not good for the channeler. While the act of channeling itself provides others with beneficial information (and therefore creates favorable Dharma for the channel), it is harder for the channeler to grow spiritually, simply because they are not present. A lighter trance has many advantages as the channel can retain much of the spiritual information.

Many channels work fully conscious at their computers, eliminating the need for tape recorders and transcribing. Through this method, they are able to carefully dictate each word for their Spiritual Teachers. Alice Bailey chose this form of channeling and wrote about it, "This whole subject has been made difficult because of the many metaphysical and spiritualistic writings which are of so low an order of intelligence and so ordinary and mediocre in their content that educated people laugh at them and cannot be bothered to read them. I want to show, therefore, that there is another kind of impression and inspiration which can result in writings far above the average and which convey teaching needed by coming generations. I say this in all humility for I am only a pen or pencil, a stenographer and a transmitter of teaching from one whom I revere and honor and have been happy to serve."[57]

Throughout my years of working as a channel I have had the opportunity to work at most of these levels, although my personal preference is voice-transmitted material, medium to light trance.

Telepathy, Clairvoyance, Clairaudience

In order for a channel to move beyond the five senses, three types of ESP must be developed. They are telepathy, clairvoyance, and clairaudience. Telepathy, more commonly known as "mind reading," allows the Spiritual Teacher and the channel to form a link. I noticed that as my ability to channel improved, the transference of information between the Spiritual Teachers and myself became stronger. The telepathic link between us had become seamless. I didn't have to go into a trance state to communicate with them. I feel their presence about and around me all of the time. This seems to be true with other channels. Clairvoyance, or second sight, is another valuable tool for a channel. This allows for mental pictures and prolonged visions to become clear and understandable. This ability allowed me to channel very detailed Earth Changes maps.

Often, Spiritual Teachers will show diagrams and technical information to assist a teaching. Technical Channels are often very proficient clairvoyants with the ability to diagram and see things that may not be recognizable in today's world. Imagine seeing a space rocket for the first time. How would you describe it? This is what Jules Verne did in his writings of 1865. "Verne's spacecraft, the Columbiad, took off from Florida and splashed down in the Pacific, where its three-man crew was rescued by an American ship."[58] However, he was not the first to see or visualize human flight. The 1488 sketches of Leonardo da Vinci envisioned air flight with a device called "The Airscrew." These two visionaries never claimed any psychic abilities, but it is clear that at certain levels their clairvoyant abilities were indeed developed.

Clairaudience, or inner hearing, is the ability to hear things not perceptible in the usual way. After the telepathic bond with their Spiritual Teacher is developed, clairaudience is the next ability that is unusually developed by the channel. This allows for the channel to hear the teacher's voice and other information that may be given. Joan of Arc may be one of history's most famous clairaudients, and she claimed that the voices of Saints Michael, Margaret, and Catherine directed her destiny.

The Harmony of the Spheres

Many channels claim to hear celestial music before or after channeling and these types of heavenly melodies have often been referred to as "The Harmony of the Spheres." Ethereal notes and choirs may have inspired Wolfgang Amadeus Mozart as a child prodigy, writing his first minuet when he was just six years old. In a letter to his father he explained, "Everything has been composed but not yet written down."[59] In just thirty-five years he composed seventeen operas, forty-one symphonies, and twenty-seven piano concertos. "Mozart never tried to understand who he was, but his ingenious naiveté was a perfect vessel for his seemingly heaven-sent compositions." Don Campbell in *The Mozart Effect* continues, "No matter how absurd and tragic his life, the channel to celestial harmony was never interrupted."[60] The Vedas, who are the sages of ancient India, clairaudiently heard the singular sounds that each planet made and claimed that if it was repeated, it would produce that planet's light and energy for the person repeating the sound. These are commonly known as bija seed mantras and they can produce healing, spiritual enlightenment, and a sense of wellbeing when properly used. A popular bija seed mantra is OM, which vibrates to the Sun.

Moving with the SuperSenses: The ONE and the Law of Love
As these three supernormal powers of telepathy, clairvoyance, and clairaudience continue to develop, this natural unfoldment leads to an expansion of consciousness. H. P. Blavatsky once commented, "A person becomes gradually ONE with the UNIVERSAL ALL," and continued to add "new senses and new powers . . . infinitely more good can be done than without them."[61]

Paul Solomon was once approached by the C.I.A. to clairvoyantly take a look (i.e., remotely view) at some Soviet files. W. Alexander Wheeler recreates the unique encounter between Paul and the agents in the biography of Paul Solomon, *The Prophetic Revelations of Paul Solomon*: "Now look, here's the principle: If I want to know what you're thinking right now, all I have to do is care more about what you're thinking than what I am thinking. That's it; that's the Law of Telepathic Communication, and as soon as I care more what you're thinking than what I am thinking, I will give up my thoughts and I will absorb yours, and I will understand you—and that's the way we're going to have to get into these Russian files. We are going to have to care what they are thinking. It's a Law of Love. You want to join me in this exercise of loving these guys in the KGB? They choked! And sent me home!"[62]

Useful Metaphors: Computers and the Information Age
Today's Information Age provides a powerful and helpful allegory to understanding channeling, the super-senses, and higher consciousness. Many channels express computer analogies when speaking about their spiritual art. Downloading often refers to time spent in Oneness with

Spiritual Teachers, with large amounts of information mentally in-fused to the channel to be retrieved later. A computer's ability to store, catalog, organize, and retrieve vast amounts of information is a helpful metaphor to understanding the Akashic Records. Almost every channel accesses the Akashic records to obtain information. This explanation and definition comes from the trance work of Edgar Cayce. "Akasha is a Sanskrit word that refers to the fundamental etheric substance of the universe, electro-spiritual in composition. Upon this Akasha there remains impressed an indelible record of every sound, light, movement, or thought since the beginning of the manifest universe. The Akasha registers impressions like a sensitive plate, and can almost be regarded as a huge candid camera of the cosmos. The ability to read these vibratory records lies inherent within each of us, dependent upon the sensitiv-ity of our organization, and consists in attuning to the proper degree of consciousness much like tuning a radio to the proper wavelength."[63] Very often a channel brings through information in a session and si-multaneously the same information is perfectly re-languaged by another channel located across the globe. The two channels may have different Spiritual Teachers, beliefs, and experiences, but the basic information is coming from the same place. My astrologer friend once told me that she thought that our current technology was only in the infancy stages of the Information Age. It is consoling to think that computers are not just technological monsters, reducing our lives to a cold, heartless control; but indeed, they are valuable teachers mirroring back to us a glimpse of our own latent, undeveloped potential. Perhaps in the future, through evolving and perfecting consciousness, there will be no more need for constant hardware upgrades, increased memory capacities, and the latest technology—our own developed super-senses will do this for us!

Universal Mind, the Internet of Consciousness

Mainframe computer servers and the Internet are insightful meta-phors to language interconnectedness, the ONE, and Universal Mind. Universal Mind operates like a huge computer server and while we are all connected to it, the super-senses of a channel can bring us into greater rapport with its benefits. After a channeled session, attendees often report a feeling of high energy, positive attitudes, happiness, and a sense of light-heartedness. It appears that channels not only chan-nel information but are able to channel a high, spiritual energy—the energy of Universal Mind. Emanuel Swedenborg, a Swedish channel, mystic, and spiritual researcher of the seventeenth century, writes about this Mind in *Divine Love and Wisdom*: "The spiritual mind, therefore, is not opened from birth, but is only in the capability of being opened. Moreover, the natural mind derives its form in part from substances of the natural world; but the spiritual mind from substances of the spiritual world only; and this mind is preserved in its integrity by the Lord."[64] Universal Mind is not bound by time or space; it exists around us, and is sensitive to our needs and desires. Ernest Holmes wrote about this concept in the first issue of *Science of Mind* magazine, published in October, 1927: "We believe that the Universal Spirit, which is God, operates through a Universal Mind, which is the Law of God; and that we are surrounded by this Creative Mind which receives the direct impress of our thought and acts upon it. We believe in the healing of the sick through the power of this Mind. We believe in the control of conditions through the power of this Mind."

Spiritual Artists, the Pioneers of Consciousness

It would appear that our positive future relies upon the art of channeling. Artistic expression has always been at the center of any revolution and why not choose a modality that speaks for the subtle and unseen realities and heralds an age of humanity's spiritual development? Only time will measure the credibility of the current group of spiritual artists in our world today. We all may fall by the wayside and history might remember this time period as The New Age Awakening and its chronicle will appear in documentaries with the likes of beatniks, bomb shelters, and hula hoops. Or better yet, all the information that has been channeled will be thoughtfully and sincerely applied and today's channel will become tomorrow's stalwart pioneer of consciousness. The Spiritual Teacher Seth, who, through Jane Roberts channeled over 1,800 sessions which are now archived in the prestigious Yale University, sums it up: "When man realizes that he, himself, creates his personal and universal environment in concrete terms, then he can begin to create a private and universal environment much superior to the (present) one, that is a result of haphazard and unenlightened constructions. This is our main message to the world, and this is the next line in man's conceptual development."[65]

"Timelessly and agelessly, the unknown poet sings,
'O, let not the flame die out!
Cherished age after age in its dark cavern
—in its holy temples cherished.
Fed by pure ministers of love - let not the flame die out!" [66]

Conclusion

I vividly remember going to see the Al Gore documentary *An Incon-venient Truth*. At the time, it was showing in only two theatres in the Phoenix Valley of almost four million people. There was no way it would ever play in my cowboy conservative town of Payson. In fact, it was already being ridiculed in the local paper under the title "Global warming theme fits agenda of liberal left." That same article used the phrase, "enviro-wackos."

The theatre was packed. I scanned nearby rows to detect any semblance of the wacko fringe left of society. All ages were present—roughly early twenties to mid-seventies. If they were conservatives or liberals, I couldn't tell. A young couple sat in front of me; they snuggled and ate popcorn.

Immediately, I sensed a connection with Al Gore. Then I discovered that we had both been raised on cattle ranches even though they were coastlines apart—he from Tennessee, me from Idaho. Our dads were farmers, too. His raised tobacco, mine raised wheat and bar-ley. Al Gore's dad was a renowned state senator; my dad isn't, but he is famous to me. I guess farm kids always feel a bond with each other. During the film I found myself distracted by a flurry of déjà vus: Sixteen years earlier I had traveled around the states with a similar slide presentation. I had even started my lecture exactly the same with a photo of the Earth, taken from space! Albeit, there were a few glaring differences—my slide show fit completely into one single carousel. Al's was replete with color animations and morphing maps. Plus, Al had slick venues, with engaging Oprah-esque crowds, while nine times out of ten my presentations were in living rooms that would later become my sleeping quarters for the night.

Still, I felt a haunting camaraderie with the former Vice President of the United States. In 1989 our lives had drastically changed: his son's near death in an accident resulted in a complete restructuring of priorities; my farm-life world torn apart by divorce propelled me into spiritual inquiry and meditation.

The first time I rolled out an I AM America Map for a family member I heard nothing but uncomfortable silence. I watched my aunt's face with interest as she poured over the map's "Bay of Harmony," which covered all of California, Nevada, and most of Arizona with water; then upward to the Pacific Northwest's "Bay of Prosperity," which rendered our beloved Idaho a new seacoast. Telepathically I was certain I heard the aforementioned phrase, "enviro-wacko," sans enviro.
I'm sure hearing me explain possible Earth Changes and the spiritual transformation that could be the antidote was surprising for my family, who had only known me as a farmwife. As I listened to Al's voice during *An Inconvenient Truth*, I sensed a similar shock in the people in the audience: he was not our President, yet he had discovered a newfound, genuine voice through global warming education.

In the midst of being labeled a chicken-little or a doomsayer, Al responded simply and elegantly, "This isn't a political issue, it is a moral one." Regarding the Earth Changes information, the Master Teachers succinctly state, "It is a lesson of change, choice, and consciousness." And both of our slide presentations—one born from science, the other from the science of consciousness—are infused with a passionate love affair with the Earth.

Three years after the first publication of the I AM America Map, Gordon Michael Scallion released a published version of his psychic Earth events in a similar map, the future United States. Within the next couple of years, the I AM America Map became totally confused with his, and the ensuing rush of dozens of other Earth Changes Maps hoped to find their places in an eager market. Soon a commercial competition of "hits" and "misses" through predicted Earth events enveloped every nook and cranny of the now sophisticated Earth Changes movement. The frenzy of pre-Y2K took over the interest of the large television networks, including late-night talk airways, and provided budding entrepreneurs and authors an abundant mercantile aimed to assist everyone to survive, "the big one."

Llewellyn Publications contacted our office in 1996. They wanted my top ten predictions for 1997—would I oblige? I called back and explained to them that the prophecies were not predictions; hence nothing was etched in stone. In fact, with greater enthusiasm I explained how this information had been given to us so that we could make informed, healthy choices that may better impact the Earth. Maybe, just maybe, this could change the outcome of the I AM America Map. I hinted at the connection between eco-spirituality and global warming, and gave my contact information if they wanted more. They never called back.

After Y2K, the overall interest in Earth Changes severely waned. People are funny—if you say something is going to happen and it doesn't, they become skeptics. We hadn't seen a decent polar shift from any predictor's forecasts, and in fact, California was still viably and visibly attached to our North American continent. In the midst of this transparent confusion, we continued to share the spiritual teachings that accompanied the map: "A change of heart can change the world."

In *An Inconvenient Truth,* the man who had served as Vice President for eight years and our nation's President-elect for one brief minute repeated what all of us—predictors, prophets, psychics, messengers, channelers, visionaries—had continuously said throughout the nineties. "Maybe now," I whispered with prayerful aspiration, "we have a chance." After the film ended, we all sat in a brief stillness. Then I heard the faint sound of two hands clapping, and then four joined with six, and soon the entire theatre erupted in spontaneous ovation. It wasn't just the sound of applause—it was the sound of hope.

It has been eight years since *An Inconvenient Truth* debuted and almost thirty since we first published the I AM America Map, and many have written or inquired, "Do you have any updated information?" or, "Is this really going to happen?" I think it is important to understand, and I've stated this earlier, that when we first began to publish this type of material, we took a very literal viewpoint regarding the prophetic information. Since those earliest years, our position on timelines and Earth Changes has shifted tremendously. Our point of view is that collective consciousness instigates a vital role in the outcome of prophesied events. Afterall, free will *is* "free" will. Every choice and action regarding our Earth and her sensitive climates and environments will play a role in the possible outcome of upcoming Earth Changes events. And don't forget that our choices blend with the karmic destiny of humanity at this unparalleled time. A Chinese proverb mirrors this thought: "Heaven has the final say." So I have no doubt that some of these changes will come to pass, and some will hopefully and thankfully, through conscious prayer, intent, and purposeful action, ameliorate or never materialize. Afterall, isn't that the purpose of Prophecy?

We've never been into dates or timelines for the changes, one exception aside. As I've said, in our early years we had no idea that the Spiritual Teachers really could not pin down accurate time frames—I guess this is because their state of consciousness resides in a non-Third Dimensional reality where the prophesied changes are not static or carved in stone. However, the Spiritual Teachers indicated that the Earth Changes could well be underway by the turn of the millennium, and we've kept that original date on the I AM America Map.

In the early 90s, after we'd discovered that the meaning of the material was slanted toward Prophecy, we discussed changing the copy. In fact, new copy was written and edited. But it didn't seem right to change it, and for the sake of transparency alongside the fact that maybe, just maybe the most drastic changes have been held back for humanity's sake, we've kept it published on the original I AM America Map. We did, however, update the I AM America Map with the publication of the 6-Map Scenario. And this series of possible outcomes of prophesied Earth Changes more closely mirrors the spiritual relationship of our double consciousness (awareness of day-to-day life as well as an etheric consciousness) to prophesied events and our susceptibility and vulnerability to cataclysmic change. In fact, it was this same I AM America Map that was given to the Indian Avatar Mother Karunamayi, when we asked her, "How bad will it get?" She smiled and responded with confidence, "We will only experience Map Number One." And now this incarnation of Divine Mother leads massive fire pujas (spiritual ceremonies) to help humanity and our Earth to heal from the dangerous potentials and consequences of global warming and climate change.

Clearly, we're not out of the woods. Perhaps we've been granted a stay—a cosmic delay, so we can evolve through the sheer grace of what might have happened, to discover the living, prescient, conscious solutions. However, I don't think it will be *that* easy. The white, foaming waters of the river of change are rapidly flowing and swiftly rising about us. Change is always challenging, whatever form it takes, and Prophecy offers an attentive and perpetual warning. If we develop "the eyes to see" and "the ears to hear" hopefully, we will be ready.

ENDNOTES

1. Stephen Knapp places the beginning of the Golden Age of Kali Yuga around 1500 AD, with the birth of Lord Caitanya (Sri Caitanya Mahaprabhu) who placed a great emphasis on congregational devotional singing and chanting the names of God to elevate consciousness and as a means for spiritual liberation. Using this timing, we have experienced 497 years of the Golden Age of Kali Yuga, approximately 5 percent.

2. The Law of Uniformity: The social backdrop of war-torn Europe, not laboratory research, set a climate that developed the scientific theory, the Law of Uniformity. After twenty-five years of revolution and war, eighteenth century Europeans sought harmony in all things, and developed convincing dialects that reflected their desire for peace. The Law of Uniformity would leave a mark upon science that would remain unchallenged for over 100 years. It is based on the idea that the geology of our planet formed within the perimeters of natural law, taking extremely long periods of time to mature and that nothing extreme or chaotic could ever occur in nature. The theory was elevated to its position by a young attorney, Charles Lyell, around 1830. Lyell sought to devoid any theory of extraterrestrial (asteroids, meteors, etc.) interaction with the Earth, and temporarily closed the scientific mind to theories based upon cataclysmic geology. Lyell's use of the Law of Uniformity painted a world aimed toward a rigid order in nature that evolved all things, inspiring one of his more famous students, Charles Darwin. [Immanuel Veliokovsky, Worlds in Collision (Garden City, New York: Doubleday & Company, 1950).]

3. www.presidency.ucsb.edu, William J. Clinton, "Address before a Joint Session of the Congress on the State of the Union," January 25, 1994.

4. Manly Hall, *Secret Teachings of All Ages*, "Pythagorean Mathematics" (Los Angeles, CA: Philosophical Research Society, Inc., 1988), page 72.

5. Wikipedia, *Divine Language*, http://en.wikipedia.org/wiki/Divine_language, (2011).

6. Frank Waters, *Book of the Hopi* (NY, NY: Viking Penguin Inc.,1963; Penguin Books, 1977), page 7.

7. Ibid., page 21.

8. Ibid.

9. Ibid.

10. Ibid., page 334.

11. Ibid., page 6.

12. Eva Wong, *Feng Shui, The Ancient Wisdom of Harmonious Living for Modern Times* (Boston, Massachusetts, Shambhala Publications, Inc., 1996), page 16.

13. William Levacy, *Beneath a Vedic Sky* (Carlsbad, CA, Hay House, Inc., 1999), page 344.

14. David Hatcher Childress, *Lost Cities of North & Central America* (Steele, IL: Adventures Unlimited Press, 1992), page 298.

15. Ibid., page 300.

16. Saint John the Divine, *Revelation 21:10* (Holy Bible, King James Version, Gideons International, Nashville, Tennessee, 1987), page 1290.

17. Ibid., *Revelation 21:21.*

18. Ibid, *Revelation 21: 22–23.*

19. Lori Adaile Toye, *New World Atlas, Volume One* (Payson, AZ: I AM America Publishing, 1991), page 23.

20. Richard Dannelley, *Sedona Power Spot, Vortex and Medicine Wheel Guide* (Sedona, AZ: R. Dannelley, 1991), page 22.

21. Ibid., page 11.

22. "The Rock Talks" (Lewiston Morning Tribune, Lewiston, Idaho), July 19, 1998.

23. "Solutions to Our Global Crisis" (Causes Newsletter, New Mexico, January, 1989) Issue No. 13.

24. Manly Hall, *The Most Holy Trinosophia of the Comte 'De St. Germain* (Los Angeles, CA: The Philosophical Research Society, Inc., 1983), page 117.

25. Lenard & Lori Adaile Toye, *New World Atlas, Volume Three* (Payson, AZ: I AM America Publishing, 1996), page 75.

26. Lori Adaile Toye, *New World Atlas, Volume Two* (Payson, AZ: I AM America Publishing, 1993), page 122.

27. www.halexandria.org, "David Radius Hudson," July 20, 2008.

28. www.ic.org, "Intentional Communities: Lifestyles Based on Ideals," August 10, 2014.

29. Paramahansa Yogananda, *Autobiography of a Yogi* (Los Angeles, CA: Self-Realization Fellowship, 1946).

30. To hold back the truth or to adorn it as belonging to an individual or group is to adulterate it. The truth then remains hidden in ignorance, superstition, and fear. Manly Hall writes in *The Secret Teachings of All Ages*, "Through education—spiritual, mental, moral, and physical—man will learn to release living truths from their lifeless coverings . . . the perfect government by which the universe is ordered. In that day when perfect order is reestablished, with peace universal and good triumphant, men will no longer seek for happiness, for they shall find it welling up within themselves. Dead hopes, dead aspirations, dead virtues shall rise from their graves, and the Spirit of Beauty and Goodness repeatedly slain by ignorant men shall again be the Master of Work. Then shall sages sit upon the seats of the mighty and the gods walk with men." (Manly Hall, *The Secret Teachings of all Ages: An Encyclopedic Outline of Masonic, Hermetic, Qabbalistic and Rosicrucian Symbolical Philosophy* (Los Angeles, CA: The Philosophical Research Society, Inc., 1988), page 80.

31. Mabel Collins, *Light on the Path* (Pasadena, CA: Theosophical University Press, a reprint of the 1888 edition (George Redway, London). Part II, No. 18.

32. Ibid., No. 21–21.

33. Alice Bailey, *Esoteric Psychology* (New York, NY: Lucis Publishing Co., 1962), page 316.

34. Lori Toye, "The Blue Flame of Gobean" (Payson, AZ: Seventh Ray Publishing, 1998), transcript page 5.

35. David Frawley, *The Astrology of Seers* (Salt Lake City, UT: Passage Press, 1990), page 38.

36. Ibid., page 48.

37. "Solutions to Our Global Crisis" (New Mexico: Causes Newsletter, January, 1989).

38. Richard Dannelly, *Sedona Power Spot, Vortex and Medicine Wheel Guide* (Sedona, AZ: Richard Dannelly, 1989), pages 19 and 24.

39. Toye, *New World Atlas, Volume One,* page 23.

40. Toye, *New World Atlas, Volume Three,* page 75.

41. David R. Hawkins, *Power vs. Force, The Hidden Determinants of Human Behavior: An Anatomy of Consciousness* (Sedona, AZ: Veritas Publishing, 1995).

42. David Frawley, *The Astrology of the Seers: A Guide to Vedic (Hindu) Astrology* (Salt Lake City, UT: Passage Press, 1990).

43. Manly Hall, *Twelve World Teachers* (Los Angeles, CA: The Philosophical Research Society, Inc., 1965), page 94.

44. "The Society of Friends." The 1995 Grolier Multimedia Encyclopedia: version 7.0.2. Grolier Electronic Publishing, 1995.

45. Ibid., "Mormonism."

46. American College Encyclopedic Dictionary: 1. (Chicago IL: Spencer Press, Inc., 1960), page 201.

47. Joseph Campbell with Bill Moyers, *The Power of Myth,* (New York, NY: Bantam Doubleday Dell Publishing Group, Inc., 1988), page 85.

48. Campbell, *The Power of Myth,* page 85.

49. Thomas Mails, *The Mystic Warriors of the Plains* (New York, NY: Marlowe & Company, 1995), page 110.

50. James Braha, *How to Predict Your Future* (Hollywood, FL: Hermetican Press, 1995), page 308.

51. Sylvia Cranston, *H.P.B.* (New York, NY: G. P. Putnam & Sons, 1993), pages 328–9.

52. Alice A. Bailey, *The Unfinished Autobiography* (New York: Lucis Publishing Company, 1951), page 36.

53. Ibid., page 37.

54. "Psychic Powers" (Alexandria, VA: Time-Life Books, 1988), page 91.

55. W. Alexander Wheeler, *The Prophetic Revelations of Paul Solomon* (York Beach, ME: Samuel Weiser, Inc., 1994), page 34.

56. Gina Cerminara, *Many Mansions* (New York, NY: William Sloane, 1950), page 23.

57. Bailey, *The Unfinished Autobiography,* page 162.

58. "Visions and Prophecies" (Alexandria, VA: Time-Life Books, 1988), page 27.

59. Don Campbell, *The Mozart Effect* (New York, NY: Avon Books, 1997), page 28.

60. Ibid., page 29.

61. Cranston, *H.P.B.*, page 226.

62. Wheeler, *The Prophetic Revelations of Paul Solomon*, page 43.

63. Cranston, *H.P.B.*, page 506.

64. Emanuel Swedenborg, *Divine Love and Wisdom* (New York: Swedenborg Foundation, Inc., 1970), page 140.

65. Lynda Madden Dahl, *Ten Thousand Whispers* (Eugene, OR: Windsong Publishing, 1995), page 183.

66. The Three Initiates, *The Kybalion: Hermetic Philosophy*, (Chicago, IL: Yogi Publication Society, 1908), from the Introduction.

BIBLIOGRAPHY

"The Rock Talks." Lewiston, ID: *Lewiston Morning Tribune*, July 19, 1998.

"Solutions to Our Global Crisis." NM: *Causes Newsletter* 13, January, 1989.

Aadhar, Anand. *The Story of the Fortunate One.* http://www.bhagavata.org, 2006.

American College Encyclopedic Dictionary: 1. Chicago IL: Spencer Press, Inc., 1960.

Bailey, Alice A. *Esoteric Psychology.* New York, NY: Lucis Publishing Co., 1962.

Bailey, Alice A. *The Unfinished Autobiography.* New York, NY: Lucis Publishing Company, 1951.

Braha, James. *How to Be a Great Astrologer.* Hollywood, FL: Hermetican Press, 1992.

Braha, James. *How to Predict Your Future.* Hollywood, FL: Hermetican Press, 1995.

Campbell, Don. *The Mozart Effect.* New York, NY: Avon Books, 1997.

Campbell, Joseph with Bill Moyers. *The Power of Myth.* New York, NY: Bantam Doubleday Dell Publishing Group, Inc., 1988.

Canty, Peter. *Eternal Massage.* 1977.

Cerminara, Gina. *Many Mansions.* New York, NY: William Sloane, 1950.

Childress, David Hatcher. *Lost Cities of North & Central America.* Steele, Illinois: Adventures Unlimited Press, 1992.

Collins, Mabel. *Light on the Path.* Pasadena, CA: Theosophical University Press, a reprint of the 1888 edition (George Redway, London).

Cranston, Sylvia. *H.P.B,* New York, NY: G. P. Putnam & Sons, 1993.

Dahl, Lynda Madden. *Ten Thousand Whispers.* Eugene, OR: Windsong Publishing, 1995.

Dannelley, Richard. *Sedona Power Spot, Vortex and Medicine Wheel Guide.* Sedona, AZ: R. Dannelley, 1991.

Dent, Harry. *The Roaring 2000s: Building the Wealth and Lifestyle You Desire in the Greatest Boom in History.* New York, NY: Simon and Schuster, 1999.

Frawley, David. *The Astrology of the Seers.* Salt Lake City, UT: Passage Press, 1990.

Hall, Manly. *The Most Holy Trinosophia of the Comte 'De St. Germain.* Los Angeles, CA: The Philosophical Research Society, Inc., 1983.

Hall, Manly. *The Secret Teachings of All Ages.* Los Angeles, CA: The Philosophical Research Society, Inc., 1989.

Hall, Manly, *Twelve World Teachers.* Los Angeles, CA: The Philosophical Research Society, Inc., 1965.

Hudson, David. David Hudson at IFNS. www.halexandria.org, 2008.

Knapp, Stephen. *The Vedic Prophecies: A New Look into the Future.* Detroit, MI: World Relief Network, 1998.

Knapp, Stephen. *Vedic Prophecies.* http://www.stephen-knapp.com, 2003.

Kozeny, Geoph. *Intentional Communities: Lifestyles Based on Ideals.* www.ic.org, August 10, 2014.

Krishnapada, Bharktitrtha. "About Vedic Prophecies." October, 2002 http://stphen-knapp.com/about_vedic_prophecies.htm

Levacy, William. *Beneath a Vedic Sky.* Carlsbad, CA: Hay House, Inc., 1999.

Luk, A. D. K., *Law of Life, Volume Two.* Pueblo, CO: A. D. K. Luk Publications, 1989.
Psychic Powers. Alexandria, VA: Time-Life Books, 1988.

Saint John the Divine, Revelation 21:10, Holy Bible (King James Version), (Nashville, TN: Gideons International, 1987).

Society of Friends. The 1995 Grolier Multimedia Encyclopedia: version 7.0.2. Grolier Electronic Publishing, 1995.

Swedenborg, Emanuel. *Divine Love and Wisdom.* New York: Swedenborg Foundation, Inc., 1970.

Toye, Lori. *New World Atlas, Volume One.* Payson, AZ: Seventh Ray Publishing, 1992.

Toye, Lori Adaile. *New World Atlas, Volume Two.* Payson, AZ: I AM America Publishing, 1993.

Toye, Lenard & Lori Adaile, *New World Atlas, Volume Three.* Payson, AZ: I AM America Publishing, 1996.

Toye, Lori. *The Blue Flame of Gobean.* Payson, AZ: Seventh Ray Publishing, 1998.

Veliokovsky, Immanuel. *Worlds in Collision.* Garden City, NY: Doubleday & Company, 1950.

Waters, Frank. *Book of the Hopi.* New York, NY: Viking Penguin Inc.,1963; Penguin Books, 1977.

Wheeler, W. Alexander. *The Prophetic Revelations of Paul Solomon.* York Beach, ME: Samuel Weiser, Inc., 1994.

Wong, Eva, *Feng Shui, The Ancient Wisdom of Harmonious Living for Modern Times.* Boston, Massachusetts: Shambhala Publications, Inc., 1996.

Yogananda, Paramahansa. *Autobiography of a Yogi,* Los Angeles, CA: Self-Realization Fellowship, 1946.

Yukteswar, Sri. *The Holy Science.* Los Angeles, CA: Self-Realization Fellowship, 1949.

LORI TOYE

Lori Toye is not a Prophet of doom and gloom. The fact that she became a Prophet at all is highly unlikely. Reared in a small Idaho farming community as a member of the conservative Missouri Synod Lutheran church, Lori had never heard of meditation, spiritual development, reincarnation, channeling, or clairvoyant sight.

Her unusual spiritual journey began in Washington State, when, as advertising manager of a weekly newspaper, she answered a request to pick up an ad for a local health food store. As she entered, a woman at the counter pointed a finger at her and said, "You have work to do for Master Saint Germain!"

The next several years were filled with spiritual enlightenment that introduced Lori, then only twenty-two years old, to the most exceptional and inspirational information she had ever encountered. Lori became a student of Ascended Master teachings.

Awakened one night by the luminous figure of Saint Germain at the foot of her bed, her work had begun. Later in the same year, an image of a map appeared in her dream. Four teachers clad in white robes were present, pointing out Earth Changes that would shape the future United States.

Five years later, faced with the stress of a painful divorce and rebuilding her life as a single mother, Lori attended spiritual meditation classes. While there, she shared her experience, and encouraged by friends, she began to explore the dream through daily meditation. The four Beings appeared again, and expressed a willingness to share the information. Over a six-month period, they gave over eighty sessions of material, including detailed information that would later become the I AM America Map.

Clearly she had to produce the map. The only means to finance it was to sell her house. She put her home up for sale, and in a depressed market, it sold the first day at full asking price.

She produced the map in 1989, rolled copies of them on her kitchen table, and sold them through word-of-mouth. She then launched a lecture tour of the Northwest and California. Hers was the first Earth Changes Map published, and many others have followed, but the rest is history.

From the tabloids to the *New York Times*, *The Washington Post*, television interviews in the U.S., London, and Europe, Lori's Mission was to honor the material she had received. The material is not hers, she stresses. It belongs to the Masters, and their loving, healing approach is disseminated through the I AM America Publishing Company operated by her husband and spiritual partner, Lenard Toye. Working together they organized free classes of the teachings and their instructional pursuits led them to form the School of the Four Pillars which includes holistic and energy healing techniques. In 1995 and 1996 they sponsored the first Prophecy Conferences in Philadelphia and Phoenix, Arizona.

Other publications include three additional Prophecy maps, ten books, a video, and more than sixty audio tapes based on sessions with Master Teacher Saint Germain and other Ascended Masters.

Spiritual in nature, I AM America is not a church, religion, sect, or cult. There is no interest or intent in amassing followers or engaging in any activity other than what Lori and Lenard can do on their own to publicize the materials they have been entrusted with.

Concerned that some might misinterpret the Maps' messages as doom and gloom and miss the metaphor for personal change, or not consider the spiritual teachings attached to the maps, Lori emphasizes that the Masters stressed that this was a Prophecy of choice. Prophecy allows for choice in making informed decisions and promotes the opportunity for cooperation and harmony. Lenard and Lori's vision for I AM America is to share the Ascended Masters' prophecies as spiritual warnings to heal and renew our lives.

ABOUT I AM AMERICA

I AM America is an educational and publishing foundation dedicated to disseminating the Ascended Masters' message of Earth Changes Prophecy and Spiritual Teachings for self-development. Our office is run by the husband and wife team of Lenard and Lori Toye who hand-roll maps, package, and mail information and products with a small staff. Our first publication was the I AM America Map, which was published in September 1989. Since then we have published three more Prophecy maps, ten books, and numerous recordings based on the channeled sessions with the Spiritual Teachers.

We are not a church, a religion, a sect, or cult and are not interested in amassing followers or members. Nor do we have any affiliation with a church, religion, political group, or government of any kind. We are not a college or university, research facility, or a mystery school. El Morya told us that the best way to see ourselves is as, "Cosmic Beings, having a human experience."

In 1994, we asked Saint Germain, "How do you see our work at I AM America?" and he answered, "I AM America is to be a clearinghouse for the new humanity." Grabbing a dictionary, we quickly learned that the term "clearinghouse" refers to "an organization or unit within an organization that functions as a central agency for collecting, organizing, storing, and disseminating documents, usually within a specific academic discipline or field." So inarguably, we are this too. But in uncomplicated terms, we publish and share spiritually transformational information because at I AM America there is no doubt that, "A Change of Heart can Change the World."

With Violet Flame Blessings,
Lori & Lenard Toye

star of David ✡ jewish symbol

Tetrahedron geometry

Merkabah star

regular star

inner wisdom — technology

#4 - Fed... Montana

In/IL

#2

#1

#3 - GA/SC

Arizona

#5

Colorado

27, 47, 56,

CPSIA information can be obtained
at www.ICGtesting.com
Printed in the USA
LVHW030846020919
629630LV00002B/316

9 781880 050507